BOSS
V**I**BES

Dale Harbison Carnegie (November 24, 1888–November 1, 1955) was an American writer and lecturer and the developer of famous courses in self-improvement, salesmanship, corporate training, public speaking and interpersonal skills. Born into poverty on a farm in Missouri, he was the author of the bestselling *How to Win Friends and Influence People* (1936), *How to Stop Worrying and Start Living* (1948) and many more self-help books.

BOSS VIBES

Timeless Secrets to Magnetic Leadership

DALE CARNEGIE

Published by
Rupa Publications India Pvt. Ltd 2024
7/16, Ansari Road, Daryaganj
New Delhi 110002

Sales centres:
Bengaluru Chennai
Hyderabad Jaipur Kathmandu
Kolkata Mumbai Prayagraj

Edition copyright © Rupa Publications India Pvt. Ltd 2024

All rights reserved.
No part of this publication may be reproduced, transmitted, or stored in a retrieval system, in any form or by any means, electronic, mechanical, photocopying, recording or otherwise, without the prior permission of the publisher.

P-ISBN: 978-93-6156-698-1

First impression 2024

10 9 8 7 6 5 4 3 2 1

Printed in India

This book is sold subject to the condition that it shall not, by way of trade or otherwise, be lent, resold, hired out, or otherwise circulated, without the publisher's prior consent, in any form of binding or cover other than that in which it is published.

Contents

1. Unleashing Your Inner Boss — 1
2. Hustle Blueprint — 19
3. Mind Power Moves — 29
4. Confidence Reloaded — 40
5. Discipline Like a Pro — 54
6. Vibe Check: Positivity Edition — 65
7. Slaying the Stage — 69
8. Hype Up with Enthusiasm — 82
9. Dealing with Drama — 90
10. Summoning Storms and Avoiding Foes — 100
11. The Warp Device — 109
12. Banishing Worries — 117
13. Optimizing Existence — 121

1

Unleashing Your Inner Boss

Fred Wilpon is the president of the New York Mets baseball team. One sunny afternoon, he decided to give a group of school children a memorable tour of the Shea Stadium. Wilpon led the excited kids to stand behind home plate, a place where few fans ever get to be. He then took them into the team dugouts, explaining how the players prepare and strategize for each game. The children's eyes widened with wonder as they walked through the private passage leading to the clubhouse, an area usually reserved only for the team and staff.

As the tour neared its end, Wilpon wanted to make it truly special by taking the students into the stadium bullpen, where the pitchers warm up before taking the mound. This would be a rare treat and the perfect finale to their visit. However, just outside the bullpen gate, the group encountered a uniformed security guard who halted their progress.

'The bullpen isn't open to the public,' the guard informed Wilpon, clearly not recognizing who he was. 'I'm sorry, but you can't go out there.'

At that moment, Fred Wilpon certainly had the authority and power to get what he wanted. He could have scolded the guard for not recognizing such an important figure. He could also have pulled out his top-level security pass, impressing the children with his influence and showing them that he had the ability to go anywhere in the stadium.

Instead of reacting with indignation or flaunting his status, Wilpon chose a different path. He respected the security guard's adherence to the rules and decided not to make a scene. By not asserting his authority overbearingly, Wilpon demonstrated to the children an important lesson in humility and respect. He showed that even those in positions of power should follow the same rules as everyone else and treat others with dignity, regardless of their status.

The children may not have gotten to see the bullpen that day, but they left Shea Stadium with a greater understanding of respect and humility. They witnessed firsthand that true leadership is not just about wielding power, but also about showing respect for others and following the rules. Fred Wilpon's actions spoke volumes about his character, leaving a lasting impression on the young fans that would stay with them far beyond their visit to the stadium.

Wilpon led the students to the far side of the stadium and took them into the bullpen through another gate. Why did he bother to do that? Wilpon didn't want to embarrass the security guard. The man, after all, was just doing his job and doing it well. Later that afternoon, Wilpon even sent off a handwritten note, thanking the guard for showing such concern.

Had Wilpon chosen instead to yell or cause a scene, the guard might have ended up feeling resentful, and no doubt his work would have suffered as a result. Wilpon's gentle approach made infinitely more sense. The guard felt great about the compliment. And you can bet he'll recognize Wilpon the next time the two of them happen to meet.

Fred Wilpon is a leader, not just because of the title he holds or the salary he earns. What makes him a true leader is how he has learned to interact with people.

The Importance of Being a People's Person

In the past, people in the business world didn't give much thought to the true meaning of leadership. The boss was the boss, and he was in charge. Period.

Well-run companies—no one ever spoke about 'well-led companies'—were the ones that operated in almost military style. Orders were delivered from above and passed down through the ranks.

Remember Mr. Dithers from the Blondie comic strip? 'BUM-STEAD!' he would scream, and young Dagwood would come rushing into the boss's office like a frightened puppy. Lots of real-life companies operated that way for years. The companies that weren't run like army platoons were barely run at all. They just puttered along as they always had, secure in some little niche of a market that hadn't been challenged for years. The message from above was always, 'If it ain't broke, why fix it?'

This old-fashioned approach to management is increasingly outdated in today's world. Modern businesses understand that real leadership involves much more than just giving orders and expecting them to be followed without question. Effective leaders are those who engage with their teams, listen to their concerns, and show appreciation for their efforts.

In today's competitive environment, the most successful companies are those that recognize the value of a well-led organization. This means fostering a culture of respect, communication, and collaboration. Leaders like Fred Wilpon exemplify this approach by treating everyone, from the highest executive to the security guard, with respect and appreciation.

The shift from the old 'command and control' style of management to a more inclusive and respectful approach has been driven by the recognition that employees who feel valued and respected are more productive, more engaged, and more committed to their work. This not only improves the overall work environment but also has a direct impact on the company's bottom line.

Leaders today are expected to be not just managers but also mentors and motivators. They need to inspire their teams, build strong relationships, and create a positive and supportive work environment. This involves a high degree of emotional intelligence, the ability to understand and manage one's own emotions, as well as the emotions of others.

Fred Wilpon's handling of the situation with the security guard is a perfect example of this new kind of leadership. By choosing to take the high road and show appreciation for the guard's diligence, Wilpon not only avoided a potential conflict but also reinforced a culture of respect and appreciation within the organization. This kind of leadership fosters a positive work environment where everyone feels valued and motivated to contribute their best.

The days of the authoritarian boss who rules by fear and intimidation are fading fast. Today's leaders are those who understand the importance of being a people's person, who can build strong, respectful relationships, and who can inspire and motivate their teams to achieve great things. Fred Wilpon's story is a testament to the power of this modern approach to leadership, and a reminder that true leadership is about much more than just holding a title or earning a big salary. It's about how you treat people, and the positive impact you can have on their lives and on the success of your organization.

The people who held responsibility used to sit in their offices and manage what they could. That's what they were expected to do—just 'manage.' Maybe they steered the organizations a few degrees to the left or a few degrees to the right. Usually, they tried to deal with whatever obvious problems presented themselves, and then they called it a day.

Back when the world was a simpler place, management like this was fine. The issues they faced were straightforward, and solutions were often clear-cut. There was little need for anything beyond basic management skills.

However, mere management simply isn't enough anymore. The world has become too unpredictable, too volatile, and too fast-moving for such an uninspired approach. What's needed now is something much deeper than old-fashioned business management. What's needed is leadership: the ability to help people achieve what they are capable of, to establish a vision for the future, to encourage, coach, and mentor, and to establish and maintain successful relationships.

'Back when business operated in a more stable environment, management skills were sufficient,' says Harvard Business School professor John Quelch. 'But when the business environment becomes volatile, when the waters are uncharted, when your mission requires greater flexibility than you ever imagined it would—that's when leadership skills become critical.'

'The change is already taking place, and I'm not sure all organizations are ready for it,' says Bill Makahilahila, Director of Human Resources at SGS-Thomson Microelectronics, Inc., a leading semiconductor manufacturer. The position called 'manager' may not exist too much longer, and the concept of 'leadership' will be redefined. Companies today are going through that struggle. They are realizing, as they begin to downsize their operations and reach for greater productivity, that facilitative skills are going to be primary. Good communication, interpersonal skills, the ability to coach, model, and build teams—all of that requires more and better leaders.

'You can't do it by directives anymore. It has to be by influence. It takes real "people skills."'

In the past, being a manager meant ensuring tasks were completed and objectives met. It was about maintaining the status quo and making incremental improvements. But today's business environment demands more. It demands leaders who can navigate complexity, who can inspire their teams to innovate and adapt, and who can build a culture of continuous improvement.

Leaders today must be visionaries. They need to look beyond the immediate tasks at hand and see the bigger picture. They must be able to anticipate changes in the market, understand emerging trends, and develop strategies that position their organizations for long-term success. This requires a deep understanding of their industry, their competitors, and the broader economic landscape.

Moreover, modern leaders must be effective communicators. They need to articulate their vision clearly and persuasively, ensuring that everyone in the organization understands the direction in which they are headed. They must be able to listen actively, understand the concerns and ideas of their team members, and foster an environment where open communication is encouraged.

In addition to communication, interpersonal skills are crucial. Leaders must be able to build strong relationships with their team members, based on trust and mutual respect. They need to be approachable, empathetic, and supportive. This helps to create a positive work environment where employees feel valued and motivated to perform at their best.

Coaching and mentoring are also essential aspects of modern leadership. Leaders must invest in the development of their team members, helping them to grow and reach their full potential. This involves providing regular feedback, offering guidance and support, and creating opportunities for professional development.

Finally, leaders must be adept at building and leading teams. They need to bring together individuals with diverse skills and perspectives, fostering collaboration and synergy. They must be able to manage conflicts effectively, ensure that everyone is aligned with the team's goals, and create a sense of shared purpose.

The shift from management to leadership is a significant one, but it is necessary for organizations to thrive in today's dynamic business environment. Those who can make this transition successfully will be well-positioned to navigate the challenges and seize the opportunities that lie ahead. The era of mere management is over; the era of true leadership has begun.

Importance of Leadership in Everyday Life

Many people still have a narrow understanding of what leadership really is. When you say 'leader,' they think general, president, prime minister, or chairperson of the board. Sure, people in those exalted positions are expected to lead, an expectation they meet with varying levels of success. But the fact is that leadership does not begin and end at the very top. It is every bit as important, perhaps even more so, in the places most of us live and work.

Organizing a small work team, energizing an office support staff, keeping things happy at home—those are the front lines of leadership. Leadership is never easy. But thankfully, something else is also true: Every one of us has the potential to be a leader every day. The team facilitator, the middle manager, the account executive, the customer-service operator, the person who works in the mailroom—just about anyone who ever comes in contact with others has good reason to learn how to lead.

To an enormous degree, their leadership skills will determine how much success they achieve and how happy they will be. Not just at work, either. Families, charity groups, sports teams, civic associations, social clubs, you name it—every one of those organizations has a tremendous need for dynamic leadership.

Jobs and Wozniak

Consider Steve Jobs and Steven Wozniak, who were a couple of blue-jeans-wearing kids from California, ages twenty-one and twenty-six. They had absolutely no business training, and were hoping to get started in an industry that barely existed at the time. The year was 1976, before most people ever thought about buying computers for their homes. In those days, the entire home-computer business added up to just a few brainy hobbyists, the original 'computer nerds.' So when Jobs and Wozniak scraped together thirteen hundred dollars by selling a van and two calculators and opened Apple Computer, Inc., in Job's garage, the odds against their smashing success seemed awfully long.

Yet, against all odds, Apple Computer became a game-changer. This wasn't just a stroke of luck or an alignment of the stars—it was leadership in action. Jobs and Wozniak had a vision for the future and the determination to bring it to life. They inspired those around them, they innovated, and they persisted through challenges that would have deterred less resolute individuals.

The story of Jobs and Wozniak is a compelling example of how leadership can emerge from the most unexpected places and people. It shows that you don't need a lofty title or a corner office to lead. Real leadership is about setting a vision, motivating others, and creating an environment where people can thrive and achieve great things.

In our daily lives, we encounter numerous opportunities to lead. Whether it's organizing a family event, taking initiative on a project at work, or volunteering for a community service, each of these actions requires leadership. It's about stepping up, making decisions, and inspiring others to join you in your efforts.

Effective leadership also involves balance. It's about knowing when to take charge and when to step back, when to push for results and when to nurture relationships. It's about balancing work responsibilities with personal life, ensuring that neither side is neglected. This balance is crucial for long-term success and happiness.

So, as we go about our daily routines, let's remember that leadership is not confined to boardrooms and high offices. It's present in our homes, our workplaces, and our communities. It's about making a positive impact wherever we are, and we all have the potential to do that every single day.

But these two young entrepreneurs had a vision, a clear idea of what they believed they could achieve. 'Computers aren't just for nerds anymore,' they announced. 'Computers are going to be the bicycle of the mind. Low-cost computers are for everyone.' From day one, the Apple founders kept their vision intact, and they communicated it at every turn. They hired people who understood the vision and let them share in its rewards. They lived, breathed, and talked the vision. Even when the company got stalled—when the retailers said no thank you, when the manufacturing people said no way, when the bankers said no more—Apple's visionary leaders never backed down.

Eventually, the world came around. Six years after Apple's founding, the company was selling 650,000 personal computers a year. Wozniak and Jobs were dynamic personal leaders, years ahead of their time. Their story is a testament to the power of visionary leadership. It shows how a clear, unwavering vision can guide an organization through its toughest challenges and lead to extraordinary success.

Corning

It's not just new organizations, however, that need visionary leadership. In the early 1980s, Corning, Incorporated, was caught in a terrible squeeze. The Corning name still meant something in kitchenware, but that name was being seriously undermined. The company's manufacturing technology was outmoded. Its market share was down. Corning customers were defecting by the thousands to foreign firms. And the company's stodgy management didn't seem to have a clue.

That's when Chairman James R. Houghton concluded that Corning needed a whole new vision, and he proposed one. Recalls Houghton: 'We had an outside consultant who was working with me and my new team as our resident shrink. He was really a facilitator, a wonderful guy who kept hammering on the quality issue as something we had to get into.'

He stated further, 'We were in one of those terrible group meetings, and everybody was very depressed. I got up and announced that we were going to spend about ten million bucks that we didn't have. We were going to set up our own quality institute. We were going to get going on this.'

He also said, 'There were a lot of different things that put me over the top. But I am fast to admit, I just had a gut feeling that it was right. I had no idea of the implications, none, and how important it would be.'

Houghton's decision to invest in quality paid off in a big

way. Corning's commitment to quality became a cornerstone of its corporate culture, and the company eventually regained its footing in the market. This turnaround was not just about new technology or better products; it was about a new way of thinking and leading.

Visionary leadership doesn't just apply to corporate giants like Apple and Corning. It's just as vital in small businesses, community organizations, and even within families. Visionary leaders inspire those around them by providing a clear, compelling picture of the future and the steps needed to get there. They motivate and energize their teams, creating a sense of shared purpose and direction.

In our rapidly changing world, the need for visionary leaders is greater than ever. Whether you're leading a multinational corporation, a local charity, or your own family, the principles of visionary leadership remain the same. It's about seeing the big picture, staying true to your vision, and inspiring others to follow you on the journey.

Leadership is not about titles or positions; it's about action and influence. Every one of us has the potential to be a leader in our own sphere. By embracing a visionary mindset, communicating effectively, and fostering a culture of collaboration and innovation, we can lead our teams to achieve great things. Balancing your work life and social life, nurturing your leadership skills, and maintaining a clear vision are key to personal and professional success. Remember, leadership begins with you. It's about making a positive impact wherever you are and inspiring others to do the same.

Houghton knew that Corning had to improve the quality of its manufacturing and speed up delivery time. What the chairman did was take a bold risk. He sought advice from the best experts in the world—his own employees. Not just the managers and company engineers. Houghton brought in the line employees too. He put a representative team together and told them to redesign Corning's entire manufacturing process—if that's what it took to turn the company around.

The answer, the team decided after six months of work, was to redesign certain plants to reduce defects on the assembly line and make the machines faster to retool. They also reorganized the way Corning kept its inventories to achieve faster turnaround times. The results were astounding. When Houghton launched these changes, irregularities in a new fiber-optics coating process were running eight hundred parts per million. Four years later, that measure fell to zero. In two more years, delivery time was cut from weeks to days. Over the span of four years, Corning's return on equity nearly doubled. Houghton's vision had literally turned the company around.

Business theorists Warren Bennis and Burt Nanus have studied hundreds of successful organizations, large and small, focusing on the way they are led. They write, 'A "leader" must first have developed a mental image of a possible and desirable state of the organization. This image, which we call a vision, may be as vague as a dream or as precise as a goal or a mission statement.' The critical point, Bennis and Nanus explain, 'is that a vision articulates a view of a realistic, credible, attractive future for the organization, a condition that is better in some important ways than what now exists.'

A vision does not have to be revolutionary to be effective. It must, however, be compelling and clear enough to inspire and guide the actions of those within the organization. Effective leaders communicate this vision consistently and convincingly, ensuring that everyone in the organization understands and embraces it. This shared vision becomes the guiding star, helping to align efforts and drive the organization towards its goals.

In many ways, leadership in today's complex and fast-paced environment is about more than just managing resources or overseeing operations. It's about creating a sense of purpose and direction. Leaders must be able to see beyond the immediate challenges and envision a brighter future. They must also be able to communicate this vision in a way that resonates with and motivates their teams.

The story of Apple's founders, Jobs and Wozniak, and Corning's turnaround under Houghton, underscores the power of visionary leadership. These leaders were not just focused on the day-to-day operations of their companies; they were able to envision a future that was radically different from the present. They communicated their vision effectively, rallied their teams around it, and took bold steps to turn their vision into reality.

For anyone aspiring to lead, these examples offer valuable lessons. Leadership is not about having all the answers. It's about having a clear vision, seeking input from others, and being willing to take risks to achieve that vision. It's about inspiring others to see the possibilities and work together towards common goals. Visionary leadership is not confined to the upper echelons of large corporations. It's about making a positive impact wherever you are and inspiring others to do the same. Leadership begins with you. Embrace the potential to lead, envision a better future, and take the necessary steps to turn that vision into reality.

Sincerity Makes A Difference

Leaders ask: Where is this work team heading? What does this division stand for? Who are we trying to serve? How can we improve the quality of our work? The specific answers will be as different as the people being led, as different as the leaders themselves. What's most important is that the questions are asked.

There is no one correct way to lead, and talented leaders come in many personality types. They are loud or quiet, funny or severe, tough or gentle, boisterous or shy. They come from all ages, any race, both sexes, and every kind of group there is.

The idea isn't just to identify the most successful leader you can find and then slavishly model yourself after him or her. That strategy is doomed from the start. You are unlikely ever to rise above a poor imitation of the person you are pretending to be. The leadership techniques that will work best for you are the ones you nurture inside.

True leadership begins with sincerity. It's about understanding your own strengths and values and leading from a place of authenticity. When you lead with sincerity, your actions and decisions are aligned with your core values, and this consistency builds trust and respect among those you lead.

Consider the leaders you admire. They are likely those who have remained true to themselves, who have not compromised their principles for short-term gains, and who have shown a genuine interest in the well-being of their teams. These leaders inspire not through grand gestures or imposing personalities but through their unwavering commitment to their values and their people.

One of the key aspects of sincere leadership is transparency. Open communication fosters an environment of trust and collaboration. When leaders are transparent about their decisions, goals, and challenges, they invite their teams to share in the journey, creating a sense of collective ownership and responsibility.

Additionally, sincere leaders are not afraid to show vulnerability. Admitting mistakes and acknowledging areas for improvement demonstrates humility and a willingness to learn. This vulnerability can strengthen the leader-follower relationship, as it humanizes the leader and makes them more relatable and approachable.

Empathy is another cornerstone of sincere leadership. By actively listening to their team members, understanding their concerns, and responding with compassion, leaders can create a supportive and motivating work environment. Empathy allows leaders to connect with their team on a deeper level, fostering loyalty and commitment.

Sincere leaders also recognize and celebrate the contributions of their team members. They understand that success is a collective effort and that acknowledging individual efforts boosts morale and encourages continued excellence. This recognition can take many forms, from public praise to private thank you notes, and it always reflects a genuine appreciation for the hard work and dedication of others.

Moreover, sincere leadership extends beyond the workplace. Leaders who balance their professional and personal lives, who show the same care and respect to their families and communities as they do to their colleagues, set a powerful example. They demonstrate that true leadership is a way of life, not just a role confined to office hours.

In the rapidly changing and often unpredictable world we live in, sincerity in leadership provides a stable foundation. It anchors leaders to their core values, guiding their actions and decisions with integrity. This steadfastness is particularly crucial during times of crisis or uncertainty, when teams look to their leaders for reassurance and direction.

Sincere leadership is about being true to yourself and leading from a place of authenticity. It's about fostering trust through transparency, showing vulnerability, practicing empathy, and recognizing the contributions of others. It's about balancing professional and personal responsibilities and leading with integrity in all aspects of life. By nurturing these qualities within yourself, you can become a leader who not only achieves success but also inspires and uplifts those around you.

A leader establishes standards and then sticks to them. Douglas A. Warner III, for instance, has always insisted on what he calls 'full transparency.'

'When you come in to make a proposal to me,' says Warner, president of J.P. Morgan & Co., Incorporated, 'assume that everything that you just told me appears tomorrow on the front page of the Wall Street Journal. Are you going to be proud to have handled this transaction or handled this situation in the way you just recommended, assuming full transparency? If the answer to that is no, then we're going to stop right here and examine what the problem is.' That is a mark of leadership.

Well-focused, self-confident leadership like that is what turns a vision into reality. Just ask Mother Teresa. She was a young Catholic nun, teaching high school in an upper-middle-class section of Calcutta. But she kept looking out the window and seeing the lepers on the street. 'I saw fear in their eyes,' she said. 'The fear they would never be loved, the fear they would never get adequate medical attention.'

She could not shake that fear out of her mind. She knew she had to leave the security of the convent, go out into the streets, and set up homes of peace for the lepers of India. Over the years to come, Mother Teresa and her Missionaries of Charity have cared for 149,000 people with leprosy, dispensing medical attention and unconditional love.

One December day, after addressing the United Nations,

Mother Teresa went to visit a maximum-security prison in upstate New York. While inside she spoke with four inmates who had AIDS. She knew at once that these were the lepers of today.

She got back to New York City on the Monday before Christmas, and she went straight to City Hall to see Mayor Edward Koch. She asked the mayor if he would telephone the governor, Mario Cuomo. 'Governor,' she said, after Koch handed her the phone, 'I'm just back from Sing Sing, and four prisoners there have AIDS. I'd like to open up an AIDS center. Would you mind releasing those four prisoners to me? I'd like them to be the first four in the AIDS center.'

'Well, Mother,' Cuomo said, 'we have forty-three cases of AIDS in the state prison system. I'll release all forty-three to you.'

'Okay,' she said. 'I'd like to start with just the four. Now let me tell you about the building I have in mind. Would you like to pay for it?'

'Okay,' Cuomo agreed, bowled over by this woman's intensity.

Then Mother Teresa turned to Mayor Koch, and she said to him, 'Today is Monday. I'd like to open this on Wednesday. We're going to need some permits cleared. Could you please arrange those?'

Koch just looked at this tiny woman standing in his office and shook his head back and forth. 'As long as you don't make me wash the floors,' the mayor said.

Mother Teresa's story is a testament to the power of unwavering dedication to one's principles. Her clear vision and relentless pursuit of her goals exemplify the kind of leadership that can inspire and bring about significant change. She didn't wait for the perfect conditions or hesitate because of bureaucratic hurdles. Instead, she saw a need, envisioned a solution, and mobilized the resources and people around her to make it happen.

Leaders like Mother Teresa and Douglas A. Warner III show that effective leadership is not about wielding power for personal gain but about having a clear, ethical vision and the courage to pursue it relentlessly. They demonstrate that true leadership involves inspiring others through actions that reflect integrity and a commitment to making a positive difference. This approach not only fosters trust and respect but also empowers those around them to strive for excellence and integrity in their own endeavors.

2

Hustle Blueprint

Dale Carnegie never penned the great American novel, but his exceptional achievements as an educator, businessman, and author of human-relations books have made him a global inspiration. His success stemmed from setting clear goals, adapting them as needed, and always maintaining a focus on his next steps.

Mary Lou Retton, a high school sophomore from West Virginia—a state not known for producing world-class gymnasts—was once a self-described 'nobody' who ranked number one in her state. At just fourteen years old, she was competing in Reno, Nevada, when Bela Karolyi, the renowned Romanian gymnastics coach who had guided Nadia Comaneci to Olympic glory, approached her.

'He was the king of gymnastics,' Retton recounts. 'He came up to me, tapped me on the shoulder. He's a big man, six three or six four. He came up to me and said, "Mary Lou," in that deep Romanian accent. "You come to me, and I will make you Olympic champion."'

Initially skeptical, Retton couldn't believe Karolyi had noticed her among all the gymnasts at the Nevada arena. 'So we sat down, and we talked,' she recalls. 'He spoke with my parents and said, "Listen, there's no gurantee that Mary Lou will even make the Olympic team, but I think she's got what it takes."'

What a monumental goal it was! Since her early childhood, Mary Lou Retton had nurtured dreams of one day competing in the Olympics. But hearing those words from the great Bela Karolyi's mouth solidified her ambition like nothing else could.

'It was a huge risk for me,' she reflects. 'Leaving my family and friends, living with strangers, training with unfamiliar faces—it was daunting. But it also fueled me with excitement. This man believed in me. Me, from Fairmont, West Virginia. I was chosen.'

Determined not to disappoint Karolyi, Mary Lou dedicated herself to training. Two and a half years later, after achieving two perfect scores, she clinched the Olympic gold medal in gymnastics for America—and captured the hearts of people worldwide.

Aim, Then Shoot

Goals provide us with a target to aim for. They keep us focused and give us a measure of our achievements.

Setting goals is crucial—goals that are challenging yet achievable, clear and measurable, both short-term and long-term.

When you achieve a goal, take a moment to celebrate your accomplishment. Then, fueled by that success, move forward to the next goal with even greater determination and vigor.

Consider the inspiring story of Eugene Lang, a philanthropist from New York City. During a graduation speech to a sixth-grade class at PS 121, Lang faced a group of children with little hope of attending college or even graduating high school. However, Lang changed their prospects with a bold promise: 'For any of you who graduate from high school, I will ensure that funds are available for you to go to college.'

Remarkably, of the forty-eight students in that sixth-grade class, forty-four graduated from high school, and forty-two went on to college. This achievement is particularly significant given that many inner-city students face formidable obstacles, with a significant percentage not completing high school, let alone pursuing higher education.

That financial offer alone didn't guarantee such remarkable success. Lang also ensured the students received ongoing support. They were closely monitored and counseled throughout their final six years of school. Yet, it was that one ambitious goal—clearly defined and attainable—that allowed them to envision a future they had never before thought possible. By visualizing this future for themselves, they turned their dreams into reality.

In the words of Harvey Mackay, the renowned business author, 'A goal is a dream with a deadline.'

Howard Marguleas, chairman of Sun World, a produce company in California, embodies a new breed of growers in the agriculture industry. His approach is grounded in setting and achieving successive goals. Marguleas observed the cyclical nature of the agriculture business—periods of plenty followed by scarcity, which were as unpredictable as they were uncontrollable, according to conventional wisdom.

However, Marguleas set out with a goal: to innovate and create new, distinctive types of produce capable of withstanding fluctuations in consumer demand. 'This industry is akin to real estate,' Marguleas reasoned. 'When the market is down, unless you offer something unique and highly distinctive, you're in trouble. It's the same in agriculture. If you're just another grower of common crops like lettuce, carrots, or oranges, your success hinges on supply shortages. But if there's an oversupply, you'll struggle. Our strategy has been to identify and seize those windows of opportunity that arise from offering something different—a niche in the marketplace.'

That's where the idea of creating a superior pepper originated. Yes, a better pepper. Howard Marguleas reasoned that if he could cultivate a pepper with superior taste compared to others on the market, wouldn't grocery stores across America want to stock it consistently, regardless of market conditions?

And so he did it, birthing the Le Rouge Royal pepper. 'It's an elongated, three-lobe pepper,' Marguleas explains. 'We were told you had to have a bell pepper, a square-shaped pepper, to sell. But once we tasted this pepper—the color, the flavor, everything about it—we knew we had something special. We understood that with proper promotion, advertising, merchandising, and branding, we could get people to try it. And once they tried it, they'd keep buying it.'

From this experience, Marguleas learned a crucial lesson: 'Never stop seeking opportunities to innovate. Don't settle for the status quo. Always strive to find ways to improve upon what you're doing, even if it challenges industry norms.'

Marguleas warns against becoming what he calls the 'me-toos' of the world—those who simply follow trends without setting their own independent goals. While they may thrive in good times, they often lag behind when challenges arise.

Marguleas hit upon a profound truth: Those who set challenging yet achievable goals are the ones who control their destinies, achieving remarkable feats.

Reebok International, Ltd., the athletic shoe company, set a significant corporate goal: to secure Shaquille O'Neal, the star of the Orlando Magic basketball team. This wasn't going to be easy, as numerous major companies were vying to enlist him as their spokesperson.

'It was a matter of convincing him that we were truly committed to him, willing to create a program that no one else could match,' recalls Paul Fireman, Reebok's chairman.

The entire company rallied behind the effort. 'We developed an advertising campaign specifically for him, even before he joined us. We invested heavily in it and put all our efforts into it. We were completely dedicated to securing him. We took a gamble. We took a risk. We invested money, time, and unwavering commitment.' Sometimes, that's precisely what setting goals entails.

'It would have been emotionally devastating if we had failed,' Fireman admitted. 'If we hadn't gone all out to bring him on board, we wouldn't have felt such a loss. But we wouldn't have had the player either.'

Goals aren't just crucial for companies; they're the foundation on which successful careers are built.

Jack Gallagher had worked in his family's tire business, taking on various roles—accounting, bookkeeping, manufacturing, and sales. His extensive experience in the tire industry taught him one clear lesson: he didn't want to remain in that line of work.

One day, Gallagher met a high-school friend who was working as an assistant administrator at a local hospital. 'That's what I want to do,' Gallagher told himself. 'I want to make a difference in people's lives. I want to lead a team toward meaningful goals.' However, several significant obstacles stood between Jack Gallagher and his goal of becoming a hospital administrator—a graduate degree in hospital administration and securing a job at a hospital, among others.

But Gallagher was undeterred by the challenges ahead. He immediately started tackling the hurdles in front of him.

He persuaded his way into Yale, secured a stipend from the Kellogg Foundation, and obtained a loan from a local bank. Simultaneously, he worked nights in the business office of North Shore University Hospital. After earning his graduate degree, Gallagher applied for an administrative residency at the same hospital.

'I met with Jack Hausman, the hospital board's chairman,' Gallagher recalls. 'I must have spent just three minutes with him, and in that short time, I convinced him. He asked me an interesting question—he knew I was married with three kids. He said, "How will you afford it? They only pay thirty-nine hundred for a resident."'

Gallagher remembered his confident response: 'Mr. Hausman, I planned meticulously before coming here. I have everything in place to support myself during this residency and transition into an administrative role afterward.'

With a clear goal in mind and meticulous planning, Gallagher pursued his ambitions tirelessly. Today, he serves as North Shore's CEO.

Neil Sedaka, the singer-songwriter whose career spans over three decades, learned the importance of setting goals from a young age. Growing up in a tough neighborhood in Brooklyn, Sedaka wasn't one of the tough guys. His earliest goal was simple yet crucial: to be liked and survive high school.

'I wasn't a fighter,' Sedaka explained. 'So I had to be liked. I always wanted to be liked. You know how it is. You're always afraid of getting into a fight.' His solution was as ingenious as it was effective—music.

'There was a sweetshop near Lincoln High School with a jukebox in the back,' he recalled. 'All the tough kids, the leather-jacket crowd, hung out there, listening to Elvis and Fats Domino. This was the birth of rock and roll. So I wrote a rock-and-roll song, sang it, and suddenly I was a hero with those tough kids. They even let me into their part of the sweetshop.'

The importance here isn't whether Sedaka's quest for acceptance from the tough kids was justified. Such concerns can loom large during high school years. Yet, instinctively, Sedaka understood how to connect with others and achieve what mattered to him at the time. For Sedaka, that high school goal evolved into a lifelong career, and his early success bolstered his confidence to aim high in the future.

Rome Wasn't Built in a Day

A similar journey unfolded in the life of Arthur Ashe, the late tennis champion who almost single-handedly shattered the color barrier in professional tennis, historically dominated by whites. Later in life, Ashe courageously battled against AIDS, raising awareness about the disease from ghetto street corners to townhouse drawing rooms. His life was defined by setting and achieving goals, starting from his early days on the tennis court.

'Breaking through that barrier, setting a goal, and achieving it, solidifies whatever budding self-confidence you might have had,' Ashe reflected in an interview shortly before his passing.

Throughout his life, Ashe operated on this principle. He would set a goal, achieve it, and then set another. Why? 'The self-confidence gained from achieving goals transforms the individual,' he explained. 'It also spills over into other areas of life. Not only do you feel confident in your expertise, but you also feel generally self-assured that you can tackle other tasks or goals using similar principles.'

The key to success lies in setting realistic and achievable goals. It's crucial not to expect or attempt to accomplish everything in one go. If reaching the moon seems daunting this year, plan a shorter trip—set interim goals.

Arthur Ashe exemplified this incremental approach in his rise in professional tennis. 'My early coaches,' Ashe recounted, 'established clear goals that I embraced. These goals weren't necessarily about winning tournaments; they were challenges that required hard work and planning. There was an implied reward if I achieved these goals. Gradually, as I attained these milestones, I found myself nearing the ultimate prize.'

Ashe applied this strategy to tough tennis matches as well. 'In tournaments, aiming for the quarterfinals or improving specific skills like backhand passing shots or stamina were my focus,' he explained. 'These smaller goals helped keep my attention away from the distant, overarching goal of being number one or winning the entire tournament.'

Most significant challenges are best approached through a series of incremental goals. This method not only encourages progress but also provides continuous motivation.

Dr. James D. Watson, director of the Cold Spring Harbor Laboratory, applies a similar philosophy in his lifelong quest to find a cure for cancer. Recognizing the enormity of the challenge, Watson and his team have set annual incremental goals, marking milestones on their journey towards the ultimate cure.

Setting and achieving goals is essential for progress in any endeavor. Dr. James D. Watson, renowned for his Nobel Prize-winning discovery of DNA's structure, emphasizes the importance of setting interim goals in tackling the complexity of cancer. 'There are so many different cancers,' Watson explains. 'Our goal isn't to eliminate all cancers overnight but to understand them step by step.'

Watson underscores the incremental approach: 'You start with small goals—understand one aspect of a cancer, develop a treatment for another—and build from there. Each achievement, no matter how small, brings satisfaction and moves us forward.'

This method of setting and meeting goals resonates across different fields. Before becoming Notre Dame's football coach, Lou Holtz faced a similar challenge with his high-school team. Undersized but determined, he memorized every position on the team, maximizing his chances to play if an opportunity arose. 'It's about preparing for opportunities,' notes writer Harvey Mackay. 'In business, learning diverse skills makes you more valuable. Whether in the office or sales, increasing your knowledge base enhances your ability to seize opportunities when they arise.'

The principle is clear: set achievable goals, incrementally expand them, and continually improve. Each accomplishment fuels the drive towards greater success, mirroring the strategies of Watson, Holtz, and countless achievers across disciplines.

Setting goals and striving to achieve them is crucial for personal and professional growth. Sometimes goals are achieved on schedule, other times they take longer than expected, and occasionally, they may not be attained at all. The key is to persistently plan and work towards them. As Adriana Bitter of Scalamandré Silks puts it, 'Maybe our goals are ambitious, and we don't always reach the pinnacle, but we can certainly start climbing.'

Without specific goals, it's easy to drift aimlessly through life, lacking urgency and direction. David Luther of Corning recognizes this challenge and actively discusses goal-setting with his children. He emphasizes the importance of self-awareness and encourages them to consider what they truly want to achieve, beyond financial rewards. 'When you reflect on your life,' Luther advises, 'what accomplishments do you want to proudly point to? What difference do you want to make?'

Creating intelligent goals requires thoughtful consideration. Luther suggests asking oneself critical questions: 'What do I aspire to be? What kind of life do I envision?' These reflections, regardless of career stage, help align actions with long-term aspirations and ensure meaningful progress towards personal and professional fulfillment.

Once you've identified your goals, the next step is to prioritize them. Not every goal can be pursued simultaneously, so it's essential to determine which goals are most important at this moment. This process of prioritization often proves to be the most challenging.

Ted Owen, publisher of the *San Diego Business Journal*, received valuable advice from a psychologist friend on how to prioritize his life goals. 'He told me to list the top ten things I want to accomplish in my life before I retire,' Owen explains. 'Then, I prioritized these goals. One of those ten became my number one priority, and so on.'

This straightforward exercise provided Owen with profound insights about himself. 'I realized that having a fulfilling, steady job, one that makes me feel good, ranked only about seventh on my list,' Owen reflects. Once you establish your priorities—your number one, two, three, and beyond—setting meaningful and achievable goals becomes much clearer and more manageable.

Goals play a crucial role both in corporate settings and in personal lives. They provide direction, focus efforts, and measure progress. Dr. Ronald Evans, a research professor at the Salk Institute for Biological Studies, reflects on how goals have evolved in his own life. 'Before I was married, I would spend weekends reading the newspaper in the lab,' he recalls. 'Research was addicting and incredibly challenging.' However, as life changed and he started a family, Evans had to adjust his habits and priorities. 'You just have to say you can't do everything,' he acknowledges.

Similarly, corporations, like individuals, benefit from clear and concise goals. Motorola, for instance, streamlined its focus in one recent year with three specific goals: to continually improve by a factor of 10 every two years, to enhance customer engagement, and to drastically reduce business-process cycle time over five years. These goals, expressed in precise terms, are crucial for guiding the company's efforts, ensuring everyone understands what needs to be achieved, and providing a metric for success.

Whether in a corporate or personal context, setting clear, achievable goals is essential. They provide a roadmap for progress, help manage priorities amidst changing circumstances, and ultimately lead to extraordinary accomplishments.

3

Mind Power Moves

I stood in line at the post office on Thirty-third Street and Eighth Avenue in New York, waiting to register a letter. The clerk seemed bored with his routine tasks—weighing envelopes, selling stamps, handling change, issuing receipts, etc. So I decided to make an effort to connect with him. I thought to myself, 'To make him like me, I need to say something genuinely nice about him, not about myself.' It was a challenge to find something admirable about a stranger, but in this case, it was surprisingly easy. I immediately noticed something I genuinely admired.

As he weighed my envelope, I enthusiastically remarked, 'I wish I had your head of hair.'

He looked up, slightly startled, but his face lit up with a smile. 'Well, it's not as good as it used to be,' he replied modestly. I reassured him that despite any changes, his hair was still magnificent. He was visibly pleased. We engaged in a pleasant conversation, and as I left, he remarked warmly, 'Many people have admired my hair.'

That person probably went to lunch that day feeling uplifted. I bet he went home that night and excitedly shared the story with his wife. And I imagine he looked in the mirror and thought, 'It is a beautiful head of hair.'

Once, I shared this story in public, and afterward, a man asked me, 'What did you want to get out of him?' What was I trying to get out of him? What indeed!

If we are so selfish that we can't share a bit of happiness and genuine appreciation without expecting something in return—if our souls are as small as sour crab apples—we will only bring upon ourselves the failures we deserve.

Yes, I did want something from that man. I wanted something priceless. And I received it. I experienced the satisfaction of knowing I had done something for him without expecting anything in return. That feeling stays with you, resonating long after the moment has passed.

There is one fundamental law of human behavior. If we follow this law, we will rarely encounter trouble. In fact, obeying this law will bring us numerous friends and enduring happiness. But the moment we disregard this law, we invite endless troubles. The law is simple: Always make the other person feel important.

John Dewey emphasized that the desire to feel important is one of humanity's deepest urges, while William James asserted that the craving to be appreciated is the most profound principle in human nature. As I've mentioned before, it is this urge that sets us apart from animals and has been crucial to the development of civilization itself.

Philosophers have debated the rules of human relationships for millennia, yet one precept stands out above all: 'Do unto others as you would have others do unto you.' This timeless principle is not new; it dates back to ancient teachings by Zoroaster in Persia, Confucius in China, Lao-tse in the Valley of the Han, Buddha by the Holy Ganges, and was encapsulated by Jesus in Judea.

Deep down, we all desire approval, recognition of our true worth, and a sense of importance in our world. Genuine appreciation, not hollow flattery, fulfills this need. As Charles Schwab aptly noted, we crave sincere praise and hearty approval from our friends and associates.

So, let's live by the Golden Rule—treat others as we wish to be treated—and extend to them the same appreciation and respect we yearn for ourselves.

The Philosophy of Appreciation

How do we apply this philosophy? When? Where? The answer is simple: always, everywhere.

David G. Smith from Eau Claire, Wisconsin, shared a story with our class about a delicate situation he faced at a charity concert. Arriving at the park, he found two elderly ladies in a contentious mood, each believing she was in charge of the refreshment stand. Unsure of what to do, David was handed a cash box by a committee member who thanked him for taking over. Introducing Rose and Jane as his helpers, she quickly departed.

'A great silence ensued. Realizing the symbolic authority of the cash box, I entrusted it to Rose, explaining that I felt more comfortable with her handling the finances. Turning to Jane, I suggested she guide two teenagers assigned to refreshments in operating the soda machine and oversee that aspect of the project. The evening unfolded delightfully with Rose diligently counting money, Jane supervising the teenagers, and myself enjoying the concert.'

You don't have to wait until you are ambassador to France or chairman of the Clambake Committee of your lodge before you use this philosophy of appreciation. You can work magic with it almost every day.

For instance, if the waitress brings us mashed potatoes instead of French fries, we can say, 'I'm sorry to trouble you, but I prefer the French fries.' She'll likely respond, 'No trouble at all' and be glad to make the change because we've shown respect for her.

Small phrases such as 'I'm sorry to trouble you,' 'Would you be so kind as to—?' 'Won't you please?' 'Would you mind?' and 'Thank you'—little courtesies like these grease the wheels of everyday life—and are also a sign of good manners.

Let's explore another example. Hall Caine's novels—The Christian, The Deemster, The Manxman, among others—were all bestsellers in the early 20th century. Millions of people read his works. He came from humble beginnings as the son of a blacksmith and had only eight years of schooling in his life. Yet, upon his death, he was the wealthiest literary figure of his time.

The tale goes like this: Hall Caine adored sonnets and ballads, particularly the poetry of Dante Gabriel Rossetti. He even composed a lecture extolling Rossetti's artistic brilliance and sent a copy to the poet himself. Rossetti was deeply pleased. 'Any young man who holds my abilities in such high regard,' Rossetti likely thought, 'must possess great insight.' Impressed, Rossetti invited this son of a blacksmith to London to serve as his secretary. This pivotal moment in Hall Caine's life brought him into contact with the literary luminaries of the era. He absorbed their counsel and drew inspiration from their encouragement, launching a career that would elevate his name to international renown.

His residence, Greeba Castle on the Isle of Man, became a destination for tourists from around the globe, and he amassed a multimillion-dollar estate. Yet, had he not penned that essay expressing his admiration for a renowned man, he might have lived and died in obscurity and poverty.

Such is the astonishing power of genuine, heartfelt appreciation. Rossetti perceived his own significance, which isn't uncommon; nearly everyone regards themselves as important, even critically so.

The potential to change someone's life often lies in making them feel important. Ronald J. Rowland, an instructor in California and teacher of arts and crafts, shared a touching story about a student named Chris from his beginning-crafts class:

Chris was a reserved, timid boy who lacked self-assurance, the type often overlooked for the attention they deserve. I also teach an advanced class, which had become a sort of status symbol and privilege for students who earned their place in it.

One Wednesday, as Chris diligently worked at his desk, I sensed a hidden passion within him. I asked Chris if he would like to join the advanced class. I wish I could adequately convey the expression on Chris's face, the emotions of that shy fourteen-year-old trying to hold back tears.

'Me, Mr. Rowland? Am I good enough?'

'Yes, Chris, you are more than good enough.'

At that point, I had to step away as tears welled in my eyes. As Chris left class that day, standing noticeably taller, he looked at me with bright blue eyes and said confidently, "Thank you, Mr. Rowland."

Chris taught me a lesson I will always carry with me—the profound human need to feel important. To ensure this lesson stays with me, I created a sign that reads 'YOU ARE IMPORTANT,' prominently displayed in the front of my classroom, a constant reminder that every student I encounter holds equal significance.

The plain truth is that nearly everyone you meet believes themselves superior to you in some aspect. A sure way to their hearts is to subtly let them know that you recognize their importance sincerely and genuinely.

Remember what Emerson said: 'Every man I meet is my superior in some way. In that, I learn of him.'

And it's often pathetic how those with the least justification for feeling accomplished bolster their egos with displays of arrogance and conceit, as Shakespeare noted: '... man, proud man/Dressed in a little brief authority/... Plays such fantastic tricks before high heaven/As make the angels weep.'

The Crucial Role of Valued Employees

Let me illustrate how participants in my business courses have effectively applied these principles. Consider the experience of a Connecticut attorney (who, due to family preferences, wishes to remain anonymous). Shortly after joining the course, Mr. R— drove to Long Island with his wife to visit her relatives. She left him to chat with an elderly aunt while she visited younger relatives on her own. Mr. R— saw this as an opportunity to gain valuable experience for an upcoming professional speech on the application of appreciation principles. He looked around the aunt's house to find something genuinely admirable.

'This house was built around 1890, correct?' he asked.

'Yes,' she replied, 'exactly in 1890.'

'It reminds me of the house I was born in,' he continued. 'It's beautiful, well-built, and spacious. You know, they don't make houses like this anymore.'

'You're right,' the old lady agreed. 'Young people today don't appreciate beautiful homes. All they want is a small apartment, and then they zoom around in their automobiles.'

'This is a dream house,' she added with a voice filled with fond memories. 'My husband and I dreamed about it for years before we built it. We didn't even use an architect; we planned everything ourselves.'

She proudly showed Mr. R— around her house, pointing out the treasures she had collected and cherished over a lifetime—paisley shawls, an antique English tea set, exquisite Wedgwood china, elegant French beds and chairs, Italian paintings, and silk draperies that once adorned a French chateau.

After the house tour, she led him to the garage. There, sitting on blocks, was a pristine Packard car.

'My husband bought this car for me shortly before he passed,' she said softly. 'I've never driven it since his death... You have such an appreciation for beautiful things, and I want to give this car to you.'

'Oh, Auntie,' he replied, touched. 'Your generosity overwhelms me. I truly appreciate your offer, but I couldn't possibly accept it. I'm not even family, and I have a new car already. There are surely others in your family who would love to have the Packard.'

'Relatives!' she exclaimed with a hint of frustration. 'Yes, I have relatives who are just waiting for me to pass so they can claim this car. But it's not going to them.'

'If you don't want to give it to them, you could easily sell it to a dealer,' he suggested gently.

'Sell it?' she cried out. 'Sell this car? Do you think I could bear to see strangers driving my husband's car down the street? I couldn't dream of selling it. I want you to have it. You understand and appreciate beautiful things.'

He tried to decline politely, but he couldn't refuse without hurting her deeply.

The lady, alone in her expansive house surrounded by paisley shawls, French antiques, and memories, hungered for recognition. Once youthful and sought after, she had built a home filled with love and collected treasures from across Europe to adorn it. Now, in the solitary silence of old age, she yearned for human warmth, genuine appreciation—and found it lacking. When it finally came, like an oasis in the desert, her gratitude overflowed with the gift of her beloved Packard.

Consider another case: Donald M. McMahon, superintendent at Lewis and Valentine, nurserymen and landscape architects in Rye, New York, shared this story:

'Not long after attending a talk on "How to Win Friends and Influence People," I was landscaping the estate of a renowned attorney. As we discussed planting rhododendrons and azaleas, I remarked, "Judge, you have a delightful hobby. Your dogs are truly magnificent. I've heard they win blue ribbons every year at Madison Square Garden."

'The impact of this simple appreciation was profound.'

"Yes," the judge replied warmly, "I take great joy in my dogs. Would you like to see their kennel?"

'He spent nearly an hour showing me his prized dogs, proudly displaying their awards and pedigrees, and explaining the lineage behind their beauty and intelligence.'

'Finally, he turned to me and asked, "Do you have any small children?"'

'Yes,' I replied, 'I have a son.'

"Wouldn't he like a puppy?" the judge inquired.

'Oh yes, he'd be thrilled.'

"Alright, I'm going to give him one," the judge announced.

'He proceeded to explain how to care for the puppy. Then he hesitated.' "You might forget, I'll write it down." With that, the judge went inside, typed out feeding instructions and the pedigree, and handed me a puppy worth several hundred dollars, along with one hour and fifteen minutes of his valuable time, simply because I had expressed genuine admiration for his hobby and achievements.'

George Eastman, renowned for founding Kodak and

revolutionizing motion pictures with transparent film, amassed a fortune of a hundred million dollars and global fame. Yet, despite his immense achievements, he, like you and I, appreciated small gestures of recognition.

For instance, when Eastman was constructing the Eastman School of Music and Kilbourn Hall in Rochester, James Adamson, president of the Superior Seating Company of New York, aimed to secure the contract for supplying theater chairs. After arranging a meeting with the architect in Rochester, Adamson sought to meet with Mr. Eastman.

When Adamson arrived, the architect warned him, 'I know you're eager for this order, but if you take more than five minutes of George Eastman's time, you won't stand a chance. He's a strict disciplinarian and very busy. Get to the point quickly and make it count.'

Adamson was prepared to do just that. As he entered the room, he found Mr. Eastman engrossed in papers at his desk. When Eastman looked up, removed his glasses, and approached them, he greeted them warmly, asking, 'Good morning, gentlemen, what can I do for you?'

After introductions, Adamson began, 'While waiting, Mr. Eastman, I couldn't help but admire your office. I wouldn't mind working in a room like this myself. I specialize in interior woodworking, and I've never seen a more beautiful office.'

George Eastman smiled appreciatively. 'You remind me of something I had almost forgotten. It is beautiful, isn't it? I enjoyed it a great deal when it was first built. But these days, I have so many other things on my mind that I often overlook the room for weeks at a time.'

Adamson walked over and ran his hand across a panel. 'This is English oak, isn't it? It has a different texture from Italian oak.'

'Yes,' Eastman replied, 'imported English oak. It was selected for me by a friend who specializes in fine woods.'

Eastman proceeded to show Adamson around the room, discussing the proportions, colors, hand carvings, and other design elements he had personally overseen and admired.

As they drifted about the room, admiring the woodwork, George Eastman, in his modest, soft-spoken way, pointed out the institutions he supported: the University of Rochester, the General Hospital, the Homeopathic Hospital, the Friendly Home, the Children's Hospital. Adamson warmly congratulated him on using his wealth to alleviate human suffering.

Soon, George Eastman unlocked a glass case and proudly displayed his first camera—an invention he had acquired from an Englishman. Adamson delved into Eastman's early struggles in business, and Eastman spoke passionately about his impoverished childhood, his mother's boardinghouse, and his determination to lift her out of poverty. Adamson listened intently as Eastman recounted his experiments with dry photographic plates, describing how he worked tirelessly day and night, often forgoing sleep for days while perfecting his craft.

Adamson had been warned not to take more than five minutes, but an hour passed, then two, as they continued their conversation. Finally, Eastman invited Adamson to his home to see chairs he had painted himself after the sun had peeled the paint in his sun porch. Over lunch, Eastman proudly showed Adamson the chairs, modest in value but precious to him for their personal touch.

The order for $90,000 was eventually placed. Who secured it—James Adamson or his competitors? From that day forward until Eastman's passing, he and Adamson became close friends, bonded by mutual respect and appreciation.

Claude Marais, a restaurant owner in Rouen, France, employed a powerful principle to retain a key employee and save his restaurant from losing her. She had been with his establishment for five years and played a crucial role in managing his staff of twenty-one. Marais was taken aback when he received a registered letter announcing her resignation.

Reflecting on the situation, Marais admitted, 'I was very surprised and deeply disappointed. I believed I had treated her fairly and listened to her needs. Perhaps, as both a friend and an employer, I had taken her presence for granted and placed undue demands on her compared to others.'

Unable to accept her resignation without a discussion, Marais approached her privately. 'Paulette,' he said, 'you must understand that I cannot accept your resignation. You are immensely valuable to me and to this restaurant. Your role here is as vital as mine.' He reinforced this sentiment in front of the entire staff and extended his appreciation further by inviting her to his home, where he reiterated his confidence in her with his family present.

Paulette withdrew her resignation, and Marais continued to demonstrate his appreciation regularly. 'Today,' he reported, 'I can rely on her more than ever. I make it a point to acknowledge her contributions and emphasize how essential she is to our team.'

As Disraeli wisely noted, 'Talk to people about themselves, and they will listen for hours.' Marais's approach not only retained a key employee but also strengthened his team's cohesion and morale.

4

Confidence Reloaded

It has been my professional privilege to critique around six thousand speeches annually since 1912, delivered not by college students but by seasoned business and professional individuals. If there's one lesson etched deeply into my mind from this experience, it is the critical importance of thorough speech preparation.

Isn't there something compelling about a speaker who clearly has a message burning in their mind and heart, eager to share it with yours? That, I believe, is the essence of effective speaking.

When a speaker approaches their presentation with such clarity and passion, they often find that the speech almost writes itself. The weight becomes lighter, the delivery smoother. Indeed, a well-prepared speech is nearly delivered before the speaker even steps onto the stage.

The primary reason many embark on this path of preparation is to gain confidence, courage, and self-reliance. Conversely, the gravest mistake is to neglect this preparation. How can one expect to quell the fears and nerves that accompany public speaking without proper preparation? As Lincoln once remarked, 'I believe that I shall never be old enough to speak without embarrassment when I have nothing to say.'

If you want confidence, why not take the necessary steps to build it? Why do some participants in this course not prepare their speeches more carefully? There are several reasons: some may not fully grasp what preparation entails or how to approach it effectively, while others cite lack of time. Let's delve into these issues in detail—clearly and hopefully profitably—in this chapter.

The Right Way to Prepare

What does preparation involve? Is it simply reading a book? While reading can be beneficial, merely regurgitating pre-packaged thoughts from a book without personalizing them will leave the audience cold. They may not pinpoint exactly what is lacking, but they will sense the absence of genuine connection.

To illustrate: I once conducted a public speaking course for senior bank officers. Naturally, these individuals, with their busy schedules and multitude of responsibilities, often struggled to prepare adequately—or even to understand what preparation truly meant. Throughout their careers, they had been developing their own thoughts, nurturing personal convictions, and viewing the world from unique perspectives. Over forty years, they had amassed a wealth of experiences and insights. However, some found it challenging to recognize this reservoir of potential material. They couldn't see the forest for "the murmuring pines and the hemlocks".

This group convened on Friday evenings from five to seven. On one such Friday, a gentleman affiliated with a bank—let's call him Mr. Jackson for our narrative—found himself at four-thirty with no topic prepared for his speech. Leaving his office, he purchased a magazine from a newsstand and, during his subway ride to the bank where the class was held, he skimmed through an article titled 'You Have Only Ten Years To Succeed.' His reading was not driven by personal interest but by the necessity to speak on something, anything, to fill his allotted time.

An hour later, he stood before the group and attempted to deliver a convincing and engaging talk based on the article's content. What was the inevitable outcome?

Mr. Jackson had not internalized or thoroughly understood what he was trying to convey. He was merely 'trying to say'—a phrase that aptly captures his predicament. There was no genuine message within him seeking expression, and his manner and tone unmistakably betrayed this fact. How could he expect the audience to be more engaged than he was himself? His speech was riddled with references to the article, with little of Mr. Jackson's own insights or passion shining through.

So I said to Mr. Jackson in a manner akin to this: 'Mr. Jackson, we are not interested in this elusive figure who penned that article. He's not here; we can't see him. But we are interested in you and your ideas. Tell us what you personally think, not what somebody else has said. Inject more of Mr. Jackson into this. Why not take this same topic for next week? Reread the article and ask yourself whether you agree with the author or not. If you do, flesh out his suggestions with examples from your own experiences. If you don't agree, explain why. Let this article be your springboard, not your script.'

Mr. Jackson accepted the suggestion, revisited the article, and concluded that he disagreed with the author entirely. Instead of trying to force his next speech into shape on the subway ride, he allowed it to grow organically. It became a product of his own mind, developing, expanding, and gaining depth just as his own children had done. Thoughts came to him unexpectedly—reading a newspaper item, discussing the topic with a friend—deepening and enriching his understanding throughout the week.

When Mr. Jackson next spoke on the subject, he had something uniquely his own, mined from his own thoughts and experiences. His speech was richer because he was challenging the article's author. There's nothing like a bit of opposition to spur one on.

The contrast between Mr. Jackson's two speeches on the same subject within the span of a fortnight was remarkable. It vividly illustrated the immense difference the right kind of preparation can make.

Let me share another example of how to do it right and how not to do it. There was a gentleman in our course, Mr. Flynn, who one afternoon decided to talk about his recent home tour. He hastily gathered his facts from a tourist booklet, delivering them in a dry, disconnected manner. He hadn't thought deeply enough about his subject. His lack of enthusiasm was palpable, and he didn't feel strongly enough about what he was saying to make it compelling or worthwhile. The whole presentation fell flat, lacking flavor and failing to engage the audience.

Two weeks later, an incident shook Mr. Flynn to his core: his motorcar was stolen from a public garage by a thief. Despite his frantic efforts and offers of rewards to the police, all attempts to recover his vehicle were futile. The police, citing their overwhelming workload, confessed their inability to handle the rising crime situation. Yet, just a week earlier, they had found time to patrol the streets with chalk in hand, issuing fines to Mr. Flynn for a minor parking offense. This infuriated him. Now he had something real to say—not from a book, but born hot from his own life and experiences. This was part of the genuine Mr. Flynn—stirred feelings and convictions that propelled him.

In his previous speech praising the city, he had laboriously crafted each sentence. But now, standing up and speaking out against the police, his words flowed effortlessly, fueled by his outrage, erupting like Vesuvius in action. Such a speech is nearly foolproof; it can hardly fail. It was experience blended with reflection.

What is Meant by Preparation

Does preparing a speech involve assembling flawless, memorized phrases? No. Does it mean gathering a few superficial thoughts that lack personal connection? Not at all. It means gathering your thoughts, your ideas, your convictions, your passions—all those daily experiences and feelings that permeate your waking life and even your dreams. These elements lie deep in your subconscious, abundant as pebbles on the seashore. Preparation entails thinking deeply, reflecting, selecting the most resonant ideas, polishing them, and weaving them into a cohesive narrative that reflects your own mosaic of thoughts and experiences. It doesn't sound so daunting, does it? It simply requires concentration and purposeful thinking.

The Sage Advice of Dean Brown of Yale

During the centennial celebration of Yale Divinity School, Dean Dr. Charles Reynold Brown delivered a series of lectures on the Art of Preaching, later published as a book by the Macmillan Company, New York. With over three decades of experience in preparing addresses and training others, Dr. Brown offered timeless counsel applicable whether preparing a sermon on the Ninety-first Psalm or a speech on labor unions. Here's a distilled excerpt of his sage advice:

Brood over your text and your topic. Let them mellow and become responsive. From these, hatch a whole flock of promising ideas, causing the tiny germs of life within to expand and develop.

This process is best prolonged, not left until Saturday afternoon when final preparations for Sunday commence. If a minister can hold a certain truth in mind for weeks, months, even a year before preaching on it, new ideas perpetually sprout forth, nurturing abundant growth. Meditate while walking the streets, during train journeys, or even in the night—though it's cautioned not to make the pulpit a habitual bedfellow, as it's a splendid place to preach, not to sleep with. Yet, there have been times I've risen in the night to jot down thoughts lest they vanish by morning.

When assembling material for a sermon, record every thought related to the text and topic. Capture initial insights and any associated ideas that arise. Write them down succinctly to fix the idea, keeping your mind engaged in a constant search for more, as if it might never encounter another book again. This method trains the mind in productivity, keeping mental processes fresh, original, and creative.

Put down all those ideas that you have birthed yourself, unaided. They are more precious for your mental unfolding than rubies, diamonds, and fine gold combined. Write them down, preferably on scraps of paper, backs of old letters, fragments of envelopes, or any handy piece of waste paper. This method is far superior in every way to using long, clean sheets of foolscap. It's not just about economy—you'll find it easier to arrange and organize these loose bits when you come to structure your material.

Keep jotting down every idea that comes to mind, all while thinking deeply. There's no rush in this process; it's one of the most important mental exercises you'll ever engage in. This approach fosters real growth in productive power...

You'll discover that the sermons you most enjoy preaching and those that truly impact the lives of your congregation are those that draw most deeply from your own inner resources. They are born from your own mental labor and creative energy. Sermons that are pieced together and borrowed often carry a second-hand, reheated flavor. The sermons that resonate, that move hearts and inspire action—they spring from the vital energies of the speaker.

How Lincoln Prepared his Speeches

How did Lincoln prepare his speeches? Fortunately, historical records provide insights into his methods. As you read about his approach, you'll notice parallels with the practices Dean Brown commended decades later. One of Lincoln's most memorable speeches, where he declared with prophetic insight, 'A house divided against itself cannot stand...' was crafted amidst his daily routines: eating meals, walking the streets, milking his cow in the barn, even during errands to the butcher and grocery, with his son at his side. Although his son sought attention, Lincoln remained absorbed in his thoughts, seemingly oblivious to the boy's attempts to engage him.

Throughout this brooding and incubation process, Lincoln scribbled notes, fragments, and sentences on whatever scraps were nearby—envelopes, paper sacks, or bits of paper. He tucked these into his hat until ready to sit down, organize them, revise the whole, and prepare it for delivery and publication.

In the debates of 1858, Senator Douglas delivered the same speech wherever he went, but Lincoln took a different approach. He continued to study, contemplate, and reflect until he found it easier to craft a new speech each day than to repeat an old one. The subject continually expanded and evolved in his mind.

Shortly before moving into the White House, Lincoln secluded himself in a dusty back room above a store in Springfield with only a copy of the Constitution and three speeches. There, free from interruption, he penned his inaugural address.

But how did Lincoln prepare for his Gettysburg Address? There have been false reports, but the true story is captivating. When the Gettysburg cemetery commission planned a formal dedication, they initially invited Edward Everett to deliver the keynote speech. Known as America's foremost orator, Everett wisely requested more time to prepare, delaying the ceremony to November 19, 1863. During the last three days before the event, Everett immersed himself in Gettysburg, absorbing the battlefield's significance.

Invitations were extended to Congress members, the President, and his cabinet. Most declined, and the committee initially hesitated to invite Lincoln. They doubted his ability to deliver a suitable address for such a solemn occasion, given his reputation in debates on slavery but no prior experience in dedicatory speeches.

Finally, just two weeks before the event, Lincoln received a belated invitation to make 'a few appropriate remarks.' It was an understated request for the President of the United States. Lincoln immediately began preparing. He obtained a copy of Everett's speech and reviewed it while sitting for a photograph at a photographer's gallery. He pondered his address during walks between the White House and the War Office, and even while waiting for late telegraphic reports in the War Office on a leather couch. He drafted rough versions on foolscap paper, carrying them in his tall silk hat. Constantly brooding over it, the speech took shape gradually.

On the Sunday before the delivery, Lincoln confided to Noah Brooks, 'It is not exactly written. It is not finished anyway. I have written it over two or three times, and I shall have to give it another lick before I am satisfied.'

He arrived in Gettysburg the night before the dedication. The small town, typically home to thirteen hundred residents, was now bursting with fifteen thousand visitors. Streets once clear were now packed with people, bands played music, and chants of 'John Brown's Body' filled the air. Crowds gathered outside Mr. Wills' home where Lincoln was staying, serenading him and eagerly requesting a speech. Lincoln responded with a few words that made it clear, perhaps with more directness than tact, that he would speak the next day. In truth, he spent that evening refining his speech, even visiting Secretary Seward next door to read it aloud for feedback.

The next morning, after breakfast, Lincoln continued to refine his address until a knock on the door signaled it was time for him to join the procession. Colonel Carr, who rode behind him, observed Lincoln's transformation from a stoic commander-in-chief to a man deep in thought, his posture slumping forward as the procession moved on. It's likely that even then, he was mentally perfecting his brief yet immortal ten-sentence speech.

Lincoln's speeches on topics that deeply moved him, like slavery and the union, wielded extraordinary power. His failures came when he lacked such personal connection. Why? Because he tirelessly contemplated and felt these critical issues. A roommate once found Lincoln in an Illinois tavern, awake at dawn, staring at the wall and declaring, 'This government cannot endure permanently, half-slave and half-free.'

How did Christ prepare His speeches? He withdrew from crowds, meditated, and fasted for forty days and nights in the wilderness. From this introspective period, he emerged to deliver the Sermon on the Mount, one of history's most renowned speeches.

'But I'm not aiming to become a legendary orator,' you might say. 'I simply want to deliver effective talks in business settings.' Certainly, we understand. This course is precisely tailored to help businessmen like you achieve that goal. Even in modest settings, you can benefit from and apply the methods of past masters of rhetoric.

To effectively prepare your talk for this course, consider these practical steps:

1. **Choose a Relevant Topic**: Select a topic that genuinely interests you or one suggested by your instructor. It's even better if the topic naturally resonates with your experiences or current interests.
2. **Narrow Your Focus**: Avoid trying to cover too much in a short speech. Focus on one or two specific angles of the subject and aim to explore them thoroughly.
3. **Plan Ahead**: Decide on your topic at least a week before your presentation. This allows time for reflection and preparation in your spare moments.
4. **Immerse Yourself**: Think about your topic throughout the day and night. Reflect on it while doing routine activities like shaving, bathing, or commuting. Discuss it with friends to gain different perspectives.
5. **Ask Questions**: Challenge yourself with probing questions related to your topic. For instance, if discussing divorce, explore causes, economic and social effects, and potential solutions. For a personal topic like why you enrolled in the course, consider your motivations, experiences, and expectations.
6. **Personalize Your Content**: For a simple topic like why you joined the course, draw from your own experiences and observations. Share anecdotes or examples without naming individuals to illustrate your points effectively.

7. **Keep It Concise**: Aim for clarity and brevity in your initial speeches. A two to three-minute presentation focusing on your topic should suffice. Organize your thoughts logically to ensure coherence.

By following these steps, you'll not only prepare effectively but also deliver a talk that is engaging and memorable, drawing from your personal insights and experiences.

When preparing a talk on your business or profession, here's how you can effectively organize and deliver it:

1. **Choose a Specific Angle**: Select one phase of your business or career to focus on. Avoid trying to cover everything in a short time; instead, delve deeply into one aspect that is compelling or revealing.
2. **Personal Storytelling**: Share your personal journey into your business or profession. Discuss whether it was a choice or a stroke of luck, recounting your early struggles, defeats, hopes, and triumphs. Narrate it with human interest, keeping it modest and engaging.
3. **Highlight Challenges and Advice**: Discuss the challenges inherent in your industry. Offer advice you would give to someone new entering the field. Address issues like dealing with labor, managing customer relations, and insights into human nature learned through your experiences.
4. **Focus on People and Personalities**: Rather than technical details, emphasize the people aspect of your business. Talk about the individuals you encounter—both honest and dishonest—and the lessons about human nature you've gained. Stories about personalities resonate more than abstract technicalities.
5. **Illustrate with Concrete Examples**: Avoid abstract preaching by using concrete examples and specific cases

you've observed. Relate these to broader truths and principles that illustrate your points. Concrete examples are easier to remember and make your speech more vivid.
6. **Consider Audience Interests**: Tailor your talk to the interests of your audience. Address their concerns and offer insights or advice that directly benefit them. For instance, if you're in fire insurance, discuss fire prevention tips; if you're a banker, provide financial advice.
7. **Prepare with Research**: If time allows, do some research to enhance your talk. Visit the library and consult resources like books, articles, and reference materials related to your topic. Use these to enrich your understanding and support your arguments.
8. **Engage with Librarian Assistance**: Don't hesitate to ask librarians for help. They can guide you to relevant materials and resources that deepen your knowledge and provide valuable insights for your speech.

By following these steps, you'll craft a compelling and informative talk that resonates with your audience, drawing from your personal experiences and integrating broader insights and research.

The Secret of Reserve Power

Preparing a speech demands a lavish and discerning approach. Gather a hundred thoughts, but be ready to discard ninety of them. Accumulate more material and information than you could possibly use. This surplus isn't just for show—it builds confidence, refines your delivery, and enriches your entire manner of speaking. Yet, this crucial aspect of preparation is often overlooked by speakers, whether in public or private settings.

'I've trained countless salesmen, canvassers, and demonstrators,' notes Arthur Dunn, 'and the primary weakness I've found in most of them is their failure to grasp the importance of thoroughly knowing their products before selling them.'

Many salesmen, after a brief overview and a sales pitch, are eager to hit the ground running. However, a significant number falter within days, some even within hours. When educating canvassers and salesmen about food specialties, I insisted they become food experts. They studied food charts from the Department of Agriculture, learning about water content, protein, carbohydrates, fats, and ash. They delved into the composition of the products they sold, attended classes, passed exams, and even practiced selling to other salesmen. Prizes were awarded for the best sales pitches.

'Some salesmen grow impatient with the time needed to study their products,' Dunn observed. 'They argue, "I'll never have time to explain all this to a busy retail grocer. If I talk about protein and carbohydrates, he won't listen, and even if he does, he won't understand." My response is, "You're not acquiring this knowledge just for your customer's benefit, but for your own. Mastering your product inside out imbues you with an indescribable confidence. You become positively charged, fortified in your mental attitude, both irresistible and unconquerable."'

Ida M. Tarbell, the eminent historian of the Standard Oil Company, shared a similar approach. When asked to write about the Atlantic Cable, she didn't settle for basic information. In London, she interviewed cable managers, studied cables at the British Museum, read books on cable history, and visited manufacturing sites. Why gather so much more than needed? For reserve power—knowing that unexpressed knowledge would enhance the impact of what she did share.

Edwin James Cattell, having spoken to approximately

thirty million people, confessed a habit: on the way home, he often regretted the good points left out of his talks. Why? He understood that talks of true merit overflow with reserves of material—far more than can be covered in the allotted time.

Preparing with surplus knowledge isn't mere preparation; it's cultivating a reservoir of strength and effectiveness that enriches every word spoken.

My dear reader, I understand your concerns perfectly. Balancing a business, family, and other responsibilities is demanding, and finding time for additional tasks like preparing speeches seems daunting. Rest assured, allowances have been made in this course to accommodate your busy schedule. The topics assigned will often be ones you've already pondered, and sometimes you'll even practice impromptu speaking—thinking on your feet—which is invaluable for business discussions.

Some participants in this course are primarily interested in developing this ability to speak extemporaneously and join in discussions spontaneously at business meetings. They might prefer to listen in class and respond to previous speakers. While this approach can be beneficial in moderation, it's important not to over-rely on it. Following the suggestions outlined in this chapter will equip you with the ease, freedom, and effective preparation skills you seek.

If you wait for the perfect moment of leisure to prepare your talks, that moment may never arrive. Instead, why not establish a specific evening each week, say from eight to ten o'clock, dedicated solely to this task? This systematic approach ensures progress and proficiency over time. Why not give it a try?

5

Discipline Like a Pro

Margaret Thatcher navigated Britain through some of the most challenging periods in its history, including the Falklands War, a global recession, and significant social upheaval. These turbulent years derailed many political careers, but as the Prime Minister—and the first woman to ever hold the position—Thatcher faced more than her fair share of criticism. Yet, one thing was undeniable: the Iron Lady never wavered. How did she maintain such resilience under pressure?

'If you lead a country like Britain,' Thatcher explained shortly after her resignation, 'a strong country, a country that has taken a lead in world affairs in good times and in bad, a country that is always reliable, then you have to have a touch of iron about you.'

According to the former Prime Minister, the formula is straightforward. Stay focused. Be self-disciplined. Have an unwavering desire to succeed. 'I do not know anyone who has got to the top without hard work,' she asserted. 'That is the recipe. It will not always get you to the top, but it should get you pretty near.'

Margaret Thatcher understood the formula for success: have a clear goal, believe in yourself, be persistent, and avoid distractions. Whether in business, family life, sports, or politics, following these simple rules significantly increases your chances of success.

The Unfathomable Drive

Ivan Stewart was a man with a goal. His lifelong dream was to compete in long-distance off-road auto racing—races spanning three hundred, five hundred, or even a thousand miles across rugged terrain, demanding hours of intense concentration and enduring backaches. However, Stewart was a general superintendent in the construction business, with a wife, a mortgage, and three growing children. He had responsibilities and commitments, and the odds were stacked against him. But he had a plan and boundless energy to pursue it.

'I wanted to be involved in racing, so I worked on the race cars after work and on Saturdays and Sundays. Then I got a chance to ride, just to be involved, never thinking at the time—not at all—that it would ever get professional,' Stewart recalls.

One day, his opportunity arrived. A driver Stewart had been working with broke his leg just before a race. The car was ready and entered, leaving no choice but for Stewart to take the wheel.

With his friend Earl Stahl in the passenger seat, Stewart set out for the race. Everything went wrong. They ran into an embankment, flipped the car, and got stuck in the mud. Other cars whizzed by, and his one chance to prove himself seemed irretrievably lost.

'By now we're the last car,' Stewart recalls of that first race. 'Everybody's gone. They start one car every thirty seconds, and there were probably sixty or seventy cars in that race. Everybody's gone. Here's Earl and me, and now we're last. We didn't go another ten, fifteen, twenty miles—whatever it was—when the throttle, this is a Volkswagen-powered car, the cable that goes from your foot back to the carburetor broke. So now I can't even drive. I said,

"Earl, get a crescent wrench." Earl gets the crescent wrench out of the toolbox, and I pull out the broken wire, and it's just long enough to wrap around the crescent. We do this pretty quickly. Within five or ten minutes, we've got a hand throttle going so I can push the throttle and clutch and drive one-handed. No power steering though. This is determination—and I want to drive.'

'I said to Earl, "I need you to shift it," because it's a four-speed transmission. "I'm going to give you an elbow every time I want to change." So I'd push the throttle, and we were so messed up—I'd have the clutch in, the throttle on, and he'd be in the wrong gear. Anyway, we got going pretty good. I'd give the throttle and lay off the throttle. I'd push the clutch in, give him an elbow, and he'd shift to a higher gear. Pretty soon, he realized what we wanted to do. We were messed up because once in a while, he'd give me a low gear when I wanted a high gear and vice versa. But we got pretty good at it. Pretty soon, we started catching up—this is a three-hundred-mile race. We catch one, we catch another. Teamwork. Yes, we got good at it. Pretty soon, we were really driving. To make a long story short, we won that race. Won that three-hundred-mile race.'

That kind of focus and self-discipline is what it takes to win the race in all parts of life.

Stewart went on to become the top off-road driver in America. He has won the prestigious Valvoline Oil Iron Man trophy—the sport's equivalent of the Heisman and Super Bowl combined—so many times that his fans now simply call him Iron Man. At forty-seven years old—ancient in this body-jarring sport—Stewart signed another three-year sponsorship deal with Toyota.

'They know I'm getting older, and there are a lot of young kids coming in.' But for Stewart, that's just another challenge, not a reason to give up. Who knows? Iron Man will probably still be racing at sixty. It's that kind of focus and determination—

whatever the field of endeavor—that separates the achievers from the non-achievers.

That's the single biggest secret to raising major money, says Thomas A. Saunders III of Saunders Karp & Company.

'When I was raising this big fund a few years ago for Morgan Stanley,' Saunders recalls, 'we had an assignment to raise two hundred million dollars for our merchant banking business. We raised two-point-three billion. It was the second-largest amount of money ever assembled for a pure equity fund. I think a lot of that success was due to sheer persistence—refusing to be deterred, refusing to accept no for an answer, and being willing to keep pushing. It was about finding out why someone said no and then convincing them to say yes.'

Fred Sievert, Chief Financial Officer at New York Life Insurance Company, attributes his perseverance to his father, also named Fred. 'The one love in his life was playing the trumpet,' Sievert says of his father. 'He played with some of the best big bands, including Harry James, Artie Shaw, and Jack Teagarden. He's a very exceptional trumpet player.'

Despite his father's exceptional talent, he never stopped practicing the basics. 'He would play scales,' Sievert recalls. 'Here's a guy who's already one of the best trumpet players in the country, and what's he doing? He's not playing some lengthy new tune that he wants to learn. He's playing the scales. Hour after hour, day after day. He would play these different scales. He would say to me that if he knew the scales and he could play them quickly, he could learn any song there was.'

That same unshakable focus propelled two Southern governors, sixteen years apart, all the way to the White House. One was a soft-spoken peanut farmer from Georgia named Jimmy Carter. The other came from a small town called Hope, Arkansas. His name is Bill Clinton.

When Carter started his 1976 campaign, few seasoned national political experts gave him much of a chance. Hardly anyone outside Georgia had ever heard of him. He faced a crowded field of higher-profile Democrats, and the campaign's first major hurdle was New Hampshire, about as far from home as this Georgian could get.

Similarly, when Clinton ran in 1992, he was considered a long shot for many of the same reasons. He was a little better known than Carter had been, but not by much, and the sitting Republican president had just won a hugely popular war.

If you believed the early experts, neither of these governors had much of a chance. By the end of the early primaries, both men were expected to be out of the running. That's not what happened, of course, and there are many reasons why. None was more important than the focus and discipline of these two campaigns.

During these grueling races, both men had many reasons to give up. For Carter, besides his utter obscurity, there was the threat of Ted Kennedy and the nagging perception that Kennedy, not Carter, was the choice of 'real Democrats.' For Clinton, there were the claims of Gennifer Flowers, the count-him-out editorials, the power of a sitting president, and a fellow named Perot.

Those odds didn't stop Carter in 1976, and they didn't stop Clinton in 1992. The biggest reason both men succeeded was their unwavering focus. They knew exactly what they wanted to achieve and worked toward a specific goal—a dream each had held since childhood. This gave them superhuman motivation. They worked tirelessly, kept their eyes on the ball, and ultimately won the prize.

Persistence is the other part of the equation. To get what you want in life, you've got to believe in yourself and be willing to keep at it. Try again and again and again.

Consistency is Chief

Burt Manning of J. Walter Thompson, one of the world's largest advertising agencies, started in the business as a copywriter. He became the only 'creative person' ever to head the company, which has produced campaigns for major clients such as Ford, Lever Brothers, Nestlé, Kellogg, Kodak, Goodyear, and Warner-Lambert.

Yes, talent and creativity are vital in a business as competitive as advertising, but without hard, well-focused, and persistent work, all that talent and creativity can come to naught. Manning learned this lesson firsthand early in his career.

He came up with what he thought was a great campaign for his first big client, Schlitz. The slogan Manning proposed was one that would become as famous as 'Mmm-mmm good': 'When you're out of Schlitz, you're out of beer.' Manning was enthusiastic about the campaign, but, hard as it is to believe today, the Schlitz Brewing Company was not. They considered the whole idea too negative and wanted Manning to come up with something more upbeat.

Manning wasn't about to give up. He went back to the client again and again, presenting the campaign a total of six times. He recalls the final reaction: 'I was able to bring it back so many times essentially because I had a relationship with this client that permitted me to and didn't make him throw me out of the room. On the sixth time he said, "All right. I don't really think this is right, but if you guys do, test it somewhere."'

The rest, of course, is advertising history. Manning's talent and creativity conceived a first-rate campaign, but it was his hard work and persistence that delivered it to the public. Patience and perseverance will accomplish more in this world than a brilliant dash. Remember that when something goes wrong.

Don't let anything discourage you Keep on. Never give up. That has been the policy of most of those who have succeeded. Of course, discouragement will come. The important thing is to surmount it. If you can do that, the world is yours.

What this means, in practical terms, is that you've got to remember what the basic goal is—whether it's selling an ad campaign, winning an auto race, or getting elected to the presidency of the United States. Then work single-mindedly toward that goal.

And be sure to follow through. That's not always easy. You have to train yourself to march through every step, to complete every detail of every job every time. This consistency makes people more valuable to a company, more crucial to an organization, and more trustworthy to their colleagues and friends—following through on every detail.

'When I walk into an office and I see a stack of return calls to be made—you know, a big stack—I think to myself, "This guy's out of control," says E. Martin Gibson, Chief Executive Officer of Corning Lab Services, Inc. 'That raises a little question about your dependability if you don't even return your calls. It's the little things.'

People who consistently demonstrate dependability are often entrusted with greater responsibilities and opportunities. 'People know they can depend on you,' explains E. Martin Gibson. 'They ask you to do something, and they don't feel the need to follow up because they trust you'll get it done. That's what dependability is about. Don't be one of those unreliable individuals who neglects returning phone calls or fails to respond to important memos from senior management. The chairman wonders, 'What's wrong with this person?'

Success or failure hinges on disciplined attention to

details—hundreds and thousands of little actions—each day. 'It's about traditional values like arriving early for appointments, honoring commitments, and taking pride in your work,' says Joyce Harvey of Harmon Associates Corporation. 'Whether it's handling a letter of credit or any task, following each step meticulously is crucial. You can't afford to skip any detail. Mistakes are costly. Take your time, check every detail, and maintain your focus.'

Attitude Goes a Long Way

Ross Greenburg learned firsthand the importance of discipline and concentration during the historic night in 1990 when Mike Tyson was knocked out by Buster Douglas. At that time, Tyson was the undisputed heavyweight champion of the world, and Douglas, although tough, was not considered a serious contender.

Greenburg, executive producer of HBO Sports, had already produced over one hundred title fights for television by the time of the Tyson-Douglas match. Despite his experience, even a seasoned professional like Greenburg can have his focus shaken by unexpected events.

'As Greenburg recalls, "In about the second round, it became apparent that something was not right with Douglas and very wrong with Tyson. Tyson had eaten three or four straight jabs, and my announcers and I immediately seized on the storyline."'

So far, so good.

'In the fourth round, Douglas threw a combination that rocked Tyson, and there was a loud scream on our communication line. Everyone in our truck started realizing what we were seeing in front of us. For one of the very rare times, we were getting caught up in the sporting event rather than focusing on our individual roles. I can remember it vividly, and all the people who work with me will tell you the same story. When I sensed this, I said, "Okay, everybody relax. Let's remember we have a job to do here. If you let yourself become too tied to the event, you'll lose sight of the work at hand." That's all it took. Immediately, everybody refocused from their visceral reaction to the event, and we resumed our duties—providing replays of the staggering combinations.'

There isn't much room for slip-ups on live TV. 'If I get caught up in rooting for Douglas at that point, I won't be able to cue up my tape machines and ads. My associate directors won't be able to cue those points so you will see that replay when the round is over, which is our job.'

But Greenburg admits that even he came close to losing his focus on that memorable night. 'I will never, ever forget—I will never, ever forget—the moment that Tyson hit the canvas. It was as if I were reading some historical account of heavyweight championship boxing, and at that split second, I saw the page turn to a new chapter and a new heavyweight champion. I'll take that memory to my grave. Tyson-Douglas, and maybe there will be another event down the line. I'll just be able to say, "I was part of that."'

Steely focus isn't important just in sports television. In the case of Dr. Scott Coyne, this same kind of focus and discipline literally made the difference between life and death.

Coyne, a radiologist who had once studied for the priesthood, was the first doctor on the scene when an Avianca Boeing 727 crashed near his home on Long Island one fateful January night. For over an hour, Coyne was the sole medical professional attending to the injured passengers. One by one, he had to tend to their injuries and soothe their nerves. With most passengers from Colombia and speaking little English, Coyne communicated with basic Spanish phrases like 'Doc-tor, doc-tor.' Despite the language barrier, he made himself understood by focusing every fiber of his being. Coyne found a way to make it work under extreme pressure.

'I had a stethoscope on,' he recalls, reflecting on that chaotic night. 'I kept saying, "Doc-tor," and some of them were crying and screaming. You don't know if they're screaming because they're scared or because they're broken apart. I was able to communicate by touching their faces. You could tell how badly they'd been hurt by how they looked at you.'

'I had to whisper in their ears. I had to maintain my composure, hold them, and try to reassure them just with my expression and touch, holding their faces. I couldn't get a history from anybody. You know, you can't ask them where it hurts: How bad does it hurt? Does your back hurt? I had to systematically check every patient from head to toe. As I moved down the row, I'd find these fractures that were just grotesque. Legs were literally hanging off. I'd examine these fractures, start IVs as best as I could, and move on to the next patient to begin the process all over again—checking their rib cage by hand. They couldn't tell me. I couldn't even say, "Point," so they could understand. It was a surreal experience because when you're in the midst of it, the adrenaline is so high.'

Focus. Intense, one hundred percent focus. That's what carried Coyne through.

His concentration was so deep that everything peripheral faded from his mind. Coyne realized the extent of his focus later when reflecting on the accident during a stress-management seminar. Others in the group recounted the expected chaos: ambulances, fire trucks, radios squawking, survivors screaming, and rescue workers shouting instructions. Coyne, however, heard none of it.

'What stands out to me is how quiet it all seemed. It was so orderly. I didn't hear a thing. I had to focus so intensely that everything else was like background noise. It felt almost like a trance. All I recall is moving in complete silence. The only sound I eventually noticed were helicopters arriving about an hour later to evacuate some of the injured.'

Focus—the ability to tune out distractions and relentlessly pursue what's crucial—that's what defined that night and helped save countless lives.

6

Vibe Check: Positivity Edition

Mental attitude. The power held within our minds. It's remarkable how a single thought can dramatically alter reality.

It might sound a bit unbelievable: 'Think happy thoughts, and you'll be happy. Think successful thoughts, and you'll succeed.' Or from the ice at Madison Square Garden, 'Convert that huge wall of hostility into a source of positive strength.' Did Dale Carnegie and Denis Potvin take a dive into the deep end together? Far from it. Both understood the profound impact of attitude. The old saying had it wrong: it's not just what you consume that defines you. You are what you think.

Contrary to popular belief, external circumstances typically don't dictate personal happiness. What truly matters is how we choose to react to those circumstances, whether good or bad.

Humor plays a crucial role. It helps maintain perspective. As Welty wisely advises, 'Keep things in perspective. When things aren't going well, take a step back, reflect, and evaluate your response. Tell yourself, "Let's reassess and approach the next challenge with a clear mind."'

There are countless things that can irritate, worry, or annoy us. But it's important not to let them. Don't allow the small things to bring you down.

'When you get cut off on the freeway, there are only two things you can do,' explains Ted Owen, publisher of the *San*

Diego Business Journal, who, like many Southern Californians, spends a significant amount of time behind the wheel. 'You can swear at the other driver and make some obscene gesture, or you can shrug and think to yourself, "How long will it take this guy to end up in the junk heap? He's not going to make it to work driving like that."'

Neither reaction will significantly impact how quickly you arrive at the office. Shrugging off these minor annoyances will get you there in a happier and more productive state of mind. It might even add a couple of years to your life.

Owen didn't always have this relaxed outlook on life. He used to have a high-tension personality, but over the years, he recognized how self-destructive it could be. When he was asked to lead the Business Journal, where he frequently comments on executive performance, he knew he needed to overcome his own attitude issues.

'Many of us tend to be reactive and overreactive,' he observes. 'Since starting this job, I've never been angry at work. I got angry other places, but I haven't been angry here.' People are responding like they've never responded before.

After years of struggle, things were finally looking up for Mary Kay Ash. She had remarried, her children were grown, and she and her new husband had saved just enough money to start a small cosmetics company—a dream she had nurtured for years.

Then disaster struck. 'The day before we were to open this company,' Ash recalls, 'my husband died of a heart attack right there at the breakfast table. He was supposed to handle the administration of the company. I don't know a thing about administration, even today. Every single penny was committed. We had only five thousand dollars, my personal savings. It sounds like very little, but today it would probably be worth fifty thousand.'

'On the day of the funeral, we had no time to waste. My two sons and my daughter and I sat down to decide what to do. Do I stop or do I go on? All my dreams just plunged to the ground.'

But Mary Kay Ash believed in herself too much to give up. Her son Richard, who was just twenty, offered to do what he could. 'Mother,' he said, 'I'll move to Dallas to help you.'

She had her doubts. 'I thought, "Big deal." How would you like to turn your life savings over to a twenty-year-old? I figured maybe he could lift boxes I couldn't. I didn't know if he could fill out an order or not. I mean, he had been just one kid that I had to bring up by myself.'

But Ash wasn't one to let doubt overwhelm her. She doesn't take well to defeat. So she pressed on. 'That was the beginning of the company. True to his word, Richard moved to Dallas the very next day with his little two-month bride on his arm. The lawyers were saying, "Why don't you go directly to the trash and throw the money in, because you're never going to make it." And pamphlets from Washington told us how many cosmetics companies go broke every morning.'

Her positive attitude got her through it all. She just kept telling herself, 'I think that people will support that which they have to create. I think it can be done, and I'm going to try.' With an attitude like that, is it any surprise that Ash succeeded?

These positive, self-confident feelings don't only help you achieve more; they also make other people want to be associated with you. We all respond to the attitudes of others. That's why people are drawn to those with upbeat outlooks on life. We want to surround ourselves with friends or coworkers who are happy and productive, who have a can-do, it's-no-problem attitude. Just as predictably, the constant complainer in any crowd doesn't get much company.

Why is this? Attitude rubs off on others, for better or worse. This is a vital concept to remember for anyone who wants to be a successful leader today. There are few more powerful motivators than a positive attitude.

We all know organizations where a large percentage of the employees are unhappy. How did they get that way? Slowly, one employee at a time. A leader has to fight that spread, constantly substituting positive feelings and attitudes for negative ones.

7

Slaying the Stage

'It's risky to charge into battle without adequate preparation or reinforcements.'

I rarely tune in to daytime television, but a friend recently urged me to watch an afternoon show aimed at housewives. Despite my initial reservations, I found myself captivated by the high ratings and the interactive segment of the show. The master of ceremonies had a remarkable ability to engage the audience, drawing out participants who, while not professional speakers and often using imperfect grammar or mispronunciations, held my attention with their compelling stories. Once they began speaking, any initial camera-shyness seemed to vanish as they effortlessly commanded the audience's focus.

Why did this work? I understand the answer well, having employed similar techniques in my own practice for many years. These ordinary men and women captured the attention of viewers nationwide by sharing personal stories—embarrassing moments, cherished memories, or tales of meeting their spouses. They weren't focused on formal structures like introductions, body paragraphs, or conclusions. Their speech wasn't polished in terms of diction or sentence structure. Yet they earned the ultimate endorsement from their audience—undivided attention. This serves as compelling evidence of what I consider the first of three fundamental rules for quickly and easily mastering public speaking:

FIRST

Speak about something you have earned the right to discuss through experience or study.

The individuals whose real-life stories captivated audiences on that television program were speaking from personal experience. They were sharing insights into topics they intimately understood. Imagine how uninspiring the program would have been if they were instead tasked with defining communism or describing the organizational structure of the United Nations. Yet, this is precisely the mistake many speakers make at numerous gatherings and events. They feel compelled to address topics they have little personal knowledge of, and to which they've given minimal attention. They might choose lofty subjects like Patriotism, Democracy, or Justice, and then after a brief scramble through quotation books or generic speaker's guides, hastily assemble a presentation filled with vague generalizations they vaguely recall from a political science class in college. Their speeches often lack substance, failing to connect these abstract concepts with practical, relatable examples that could engage their audience.

At an area meeting of Dale Carnegie instructors in the Conrad Hilton Hotel in Chicago some years ago, a student speaker began with a grand proclamation: 'Liberty, Equality, Fraternity. These are the mightiest ideas in the dictionary of mankind. Without liberty, life is not worth living. Imagine what existence would be like if your freedom of action would be restricted on all sides.'

But his speech was abruptly halted by the instructor, who wisely questioned the basis of his assertions. The instructor wanted to know why the student held these beliefs and whether he could substantiate them with personal experience or evidence. What followed was a remarkable story.

The student revealed himself as a former French underground fighter who had endured severe hardships under Nazi occupation. He vividly recounted the injustices suffered by his family, his daring escape from the secret police, and his eventual journey to America. He concluded with a poignant reflection: 'As I walked down Michigan Avenue to this hotel today, I was free to come and go as I wished. I passed a policeman who paid me no mind. I entered this hotel without needing to show identification, and when this meeting ends, I can go anywhere in Chicago I choose. Believe me, freedom is worth fighting for.'

His heartfelt narrative resonated deeply with the audience, who responded with a standing ovation.

'Tell us what life has taught you.'

Speakers who delve into personal lessons learned invariably captivate their audience. From my own experience, convincing speakers to embrace this approach can be a challenge—they often view personal anecdotes as too mundane or limiting. Instead, they prefer to discuss lofty concepts and philosophical ideas, where the air is thin and difficult for ordinary listeners to grasp. They provide editorials when what we crave is real, relatable news.

Yet, none of us mind hearing editorials when they come from someone who has earned the right to opine—a seasoned editor or a respected publisher. The essence, however, lies in this: Speak about what life has taught you, and I'll hang on every word. Emerson was known for his willingness to listen to anyone, regardless of their background, believing he could glean wisdom from every encounter.

Having listened to countless speeches across varied settings, I can honestly say I've never found a talk dull when the speaker shares what life has taught them, no matter how seemingly insignificant the lesson might appear.

To illustrate: Several years ago, a member of our instructional team led a public speaking course for senior officers from New York City banks. Naturally, these individuals, with their busy schedules and numerous responsibilities, often struggled to adequately prepare—or even to conceptualize what preparation entailed. Throughout their lives, they had been immersed in their own thoughts, developing personal convictions, viewing things from unique perspectives, and accumulating a wealth of personal experiences. They had spent four decades amassing material for speeches. But for some, this realization was challenging.

One particular Friday, a gentleman affiliated with an uptown bank—we'll refer to him as Mr. Jackson for our narrative—found himself at 4:30 PM with the daunting task of preparing a talk. He left his office, purchased a copy of *Forbes' Magazine* at a nearby newsstand, and read an article titled, 'You Have Only Ten Years to Succeed' during his subway ride down to the Federal Reserve Bank where the class was held. He wasn't particularly interested in the article itself; he simply needed something to speak about to fill his allotted time.

An hour later, he stood up to deliver his speech, attempting to convey the contents of the article convincingly and engagingly. What happened next was inevitable.

He hadn't truly internalized or understood what he was trying to communicate. The phrase 'trying to say' perfectly encapsulates his predicament. There was no genuine message bursting forth from within him; instead, he was struggling. His demeanor and tone unmistakably betrayed his lack of conviction. How could he expect the audience to be moved when he himself wasn't? He leaned heavily on references to the article, citing what the author had said. It was filled with *Forbes' Magazine* content, but sadly lacking in Mr. Jackson's personal perspective.

After he concluded his speech, the instructor intervened,

stating, 'Mr. Jackson, we are not interested in the shadowy personality behind that article. He isn't here; we can't see him. What we are interested in is you and your ideas. Speak to us from your personal perspective, not someone else's. Inject more of yourself, more of Mr. Jackson, into your presentation. Would you consider revisiting this topic next week? Re-read the article and ask yourself whether you agree with the author or not. If you do, illustrate your agreement with examples from your own experiences. If you disagree, explain why. Let this article serve as a springboard for your own unique insights.'

Mr. Jackson took the instructor's advice to heart. Upon rereading the article, he found himself in complete disagreement with the author. Drawing from his extensive experience as a bank executive, he delved deep into his memory to gather examples that substantiated his points of disagreement. He crafted his ideas with rich details and anecdotes from his own professional background.

When Mr. Jackson returned the following week, he delivered a speech brimming with his personal convictions and insights. Instead of regurgitating a magazine article, he shared original perspectives and real-world experiences. His talk resonated with authenticity, offering fresh perspectives and genuine insights that stemmed from his own unique perspective and expertise.

It's clear that Mr. Jackson's transformed approach left a profound impact on the class. By injecting his own voice and experiences into his presentation, he not only captivated his audience but also demonstrated the power of personal authenticity and depth of knowledge. His speech, crafted from his own 'mint,' undoubtedly made a stronger and lasting impression compared to his previous attempt.

Seek Topics Rooted in Your Experience

During a gathering of our instructors, they were tasked with jotting down the most common issue they faced with novice speakers. Upon tallying the responses, it became evident that 'helping beginners find the right topic' was the predominant challenge encountered during the early stages of our course.

But what defines the right topic? It's one that resonates deeply with you, a subject you have lived through, internalized, and reflected upon. How does one discover such topics? By delving into your memories and exploring your personal history for those significant moments that have left a lasting impact on you.

Several years ago, we conducted a study to identify topics that consistently captured the attention of our class audiences. We discovered that the most engaging topics typically revolved around specific, well-defined aspects of one's personal background:

Childhood Memories and Upbringing: Engaging Topics for Speaking

Topics centered around early years—family dynamics, childhood memories, and school experiences—are inherently captivating because they offer insights into how individuals navigate and overcome challenges in their upbringing.

Whenever you have the opportunity, weave illustrations and examples from your own early life into your talks. The enduring popularity of plays, movies, and stories that explore the theme of overcoming childhood obstacles underscores the universal appeal of this subject matter.

But how can you be certain others will find your childhood experiences interesting? There's a straightforward litmus test: if a particular memory remains vivid in your mind after many years, it's likely to resonate with an audience.

Early Struggles to Get Ahead: A Compelling Topic

Exploring the early struggles to establish oneself in the world is a rich source of human interest. Audiences are captivated by stories of how individuals made their initial marks in their professions or careers. Share your experiences of entering a particular job or profession, recount the twists of fate that shaped your path, and reflect on the setbacks, hopes, and triumphs encountered along the way.

Nearly everyone's journey through life, when narrated with humility, provides compelling material that resonates with others.

Hobbies and Recreation: Sharing Personal Passions

Topics related to hobbies and recreation are inherently engaging because they stem from personal interests and choices. When you speak about something you genuinely enjoy, your natural enthusiasm shines through and captures the audience's attention effortlessly. Whether it's a hobby, a recreational activity, or a passion pursuit, discussing what brings you joy and fulfillment is a surefire way to connect with any audience.

Special Areas of Knowledge: Sharing Expertise

After years of dedicated work in your field, you've likely become an expert in your line of endeavor. When you discuss aspects of your job or profession based on your extensive experience or study, you can be sure of garnering respectful attention from your audience.

Unusual Experiences: Compelling Speech Material

Have you encountered extraordinary situations, such as meeting a prominent figure, facing combat, or navigating a profound spiritual crisis? These experiences often provide the most captivating material for speeches. They offer unique insights and personal reflections that resonate deeply with listeners.

Beliefs and Convictions: Speaking from Deep Understanding

If you've invested substantial time and effort contemplating critical global issues, you've earned the right to share your beliefs and convictions. However, ensure your talk is grounded in specific examples and instances that illustrate your viewpoints. Avoid relying solely on generalizations or superficial knowledge gained from casual reading. If your understanding of a subject matches or exceeds that of your audience, delve into it confidently. Conversely, if your expertise is limited, it's wise to choose another topic.

When you speak from a place of genuine expertise or profound personal experience, your speech is not only informative but also deeply engaging for your audience.

Preparing a speech isn't simply about jotting down mechanical words or memorizing phrases. It's not about regurgitating ideas borrowed hastily from books or articles. Instead, it involves delving into the depths of your mind and heart to articulate the core convictions that life has etched there. Never doubt that this material exists within you—it does, richly stored and waiting to be unearthed.

Don't dismiss such material as too personal or insignificant for an audience. I've personally found great entertainment and profound emotional impact in speeches filled with such genuine, heartfelt content—more so than many delivered by professional speakers.

SECOND

Ensure You Are Enthusiastic About Your Topic

Not all topics that we are knowledgeable about excite us. For example, as a do-it-yourself enthusiast, I may be qualified to discuss washing dishes, but I find little excitement in the topic. In contrast, I've heard homemakers—efficient managers of households—deliver captivating speeches on the very same subject. They've managed to stir up a passionate frustration about the perpetual task of washing dishes, or they've devised ingenious ways to navigate around this mundane chore, thereby genuinely becoming enthusiastic about it. Consequently, they've been able to speak effectively on this seemingly mundane topic.

Here's a litmus test to gauge the suitability of a topic you're considering for a public speech: If someone were to challenge your viewpoint directly, would you feel compelled to passionately and earnestly defend your position? If so, then you've likely found the right subject for you.

Recently, I rediscovered some notes from 1926, reflecting on my visit to the Seventh Session of the League of Nations in Geneva, Switzerland. In those notes, I described how several speakers delivered lifeless speeches reading from manuscripts, until Sir George Foster of Canada took the floor. Unlike the others, he spoke without any notes, gesturing passionately throughout. His sincerity and conviction were palpable—he genuinely wanted to convey his cherished beliefs to the audience. This experience reinforced principles I emphasize in my teaching.

I often reminisce about Sir George's speech. His sincerity

and earnestness exemplified the importance of choosing topics that resonate deeply within, not just intellectually. Bishop Fulton J. Sheen, renowned for his dynamic speaking, learned this invaluable lesson early in life.

'I was chosen for the debating team in college,' he recounted in his book, *Life Is Worth Living*, 'and the night before the Notre Dame debate, our professor of debating called me to his office and scolded me.'

'"You are absolutely rotten. We have never had anybody in the history of this college who was a worse speaker than yourself."'

'"Well," I said, trying to justify myself, "if I am so rotten why did you pick me for the team?"'

'"Because," he answered, "you can think; not because you can talk. Get over in that corner. Take a paragraph of your speech and go through it." I repeated a paragraph over and over again for an hour, at the end of which he said, 'Do you see any mistake in that?"

'"No." Again an hour and a half, two hours, two and a half hours, at the end of which I was exhausted. He said, "Do you still not see what is wrong?"'

'After two and a half hours, my quick mind finally caught on. I realized, "Yes, I am not sincere. I am not being myself. I do not speak as if I truly mean it."' At that moment, Bishop Sheen learned a lesson he would never forget: he began to inject his own passion into his speeches. Only then did the wise professor nod and say, 'Now, you are ready to speak!'

When a member of our classes says, 'I don't get excited about anything; I lead a humdrum sort of life,' our instructors are trained to inquire about their hobbies and interests. One may enjoy movies, another bowling, and another cultivating roses. One man even shared his passion for collecting matchbooks.

As the instructor probed further into this unique hobby, the man gradually became animated. Gesturing enthusiastically, he described the elaborate cabinets where he stored his collection, boasting of matchbooks from nearly every country in the world. It was when he became excited about his favorite topic that the instructor interrupted him.

'Why don't you tell us about this subject? It sounds fascinating to me.' He responded with doubt, saying he didn't think anyone would find it interesting. Here was a man who had dedicated years to a hobby that was almost a passion for him, yet he doubted its value as a speaking topic. The instructor assured him that the true gauge of interest in a subject lies in the speaker's own enthusiasm for it. That evening, he spoke with all the fervor of a dedicated collector, and later gained local recognition by presenting on matchbook collecting at various luncheon clubs.

This example directly leads us to the third guiding principle for those seeking a quick and effective path to public speaking.

THIRD

Be Eager to Share Your Talk with Your Listeners

Every speaking situation involves three elements: the speaker, the speech or message, and the audience. The first two principles discussed the relationship between the speaker and their speech. However, until the speaker engages with a live audience, there is no true speaking situation. A well-prepared speech on a topic that excites the speaker is essential, but for complete success, another element is crucial during delivery. The speaker must convey to the audience that their message is vital and relevant. They must not only be enthusiastic about their topic but also eager to transmit this enthusiasm to their listeners.

Throughout history, effective public speakers have possessed a quality akin to salesmanship or evangelism. They earnestly desire their audience to empathize with their perspective, to take action as they suggest, and to share in their experiences. Such speakers are audience-centered, not self-centered. They understand that the success or failure of their talk rests not with them, but in the minds and hearts of their listeners.

I trained several men at the New York City Chapter of the American Institute of Banking to speak during a thrift campaign. One man, in particular, struggled to connect with his audience. The first step in helping him was to ignite his passion and enthusiasm for his subject. I advised him to spend time alone, reflecting deeply on the importance of the issue. I urged him to consider the sobering statistics from the Probate Court Records in New York: over 85 percent of people leave nothing at death, with only 3.3 percent leaving substantial legacies of $10,000 or more. He needed to internalize the notion that he was not asking for favors but preparing people for financial security in their old age and ensuring their families' welfare.

I encouraged him to see himself as performing a vital social service, akin to a crusader on a mission. He contemplated these facts earnestly, letting them kindle his interest and enthusiasm. He came to feel deeply that he had a mission to fulfill. When he finally spoke, his words rang with conviction. He effectively persuaded his audience about the benefits of thrift because he genuinely wanted to help people. No longer just reciting facts, he became a missionary, passionately seeking to win converts to a cause he believed in wholeheartedly.

At one point in my teaching career, I heavily relied on the textbook rules of public speaking. In doing so, I unwittingly perpetuated the same rigid practices that had been imposed on me by teachers rooted in the formalities of elocution.

I vividly recall my initial lessons in speaking, where I was instructed to keep my arm hanging loosely at my side, palm facing backward, fingers half-closed, and thumb touching my leg. I was drilled to raise my arm in a graceful curve, perform a classical wrist turn, and then unfold my fingers one by one—first the forefinger, then the second finger, and finally the little finger. After this elaborate and ornamental movement, the arm was to retrace its path and return to rest beside the leg. The entire process felt stiff and contrived, devoid of any genuine connection or authenticity.

My instructor never encouraged me to inject my own personality into my speaking, nor did he foster a natural, lively interaction with the audience as one would in a dynamic conversation.

Compare this mechanical approach to speech training with the three fundamental principles I have been discussing in this chapter. These principles form the cornerstone of my entire approach to effective speaking training, and you will encounter them repeatedly throughout this book.

8

Hype Up with Enthusiasm

If you find yourself addressing a group of scientists on subjects like the intricacies of butterfly wing veins or road structure, it's unlikely to stir deep emotions in either you or your audience. These topics are purely intellectual. However, if your aim is to persuade men to support a cause like abolishing child labor or to inspire them to fight for freedom, you must appeal directly to their emotions. We lie on comfortable beds, sit close to the radiator on cold days, indulge in cherry pie, and pursue romantic interests not because we've reasoned it out as the right thing to do, but because it feels right. No one follows a diet solely based on a chart; our emotions guide our choices and behaviors. Humans are creatures driven by feelings, thus a public speaker's ability to move people to action hinges largely on their capacity to touch those emotions.

Historically, some of America's most powerful speeches were ignited by the anguish of African American mothers witnessing their children sold into slavery on auction blocks. These mothers lacked formal speaking skills but possessed something far more potent than technique: raw emotion. Throughout history, enduring speeches haven't centered on economic policies or governmental appropriations. Instead, they've resonated with emotional intensity. Prosperity and peace seldom inspire profound eloquence; it's in times of great injustice, when public sentiment burns with fervor, that speeches become unforgettable. Patrick Henry delivered an immortal address during such a crisis, passionately advocating for liberty with his famous words, 'Give me liberty or give me death.' Had he lived in a different era, arguing for judicial reforms, his legacy would likely have been quite different.

Political parties often invest in bands and applause to stir up enthusiasm, arguing that emotional appeal is more effective than reasoned arguments in securing votes. The validity of this approach depends on the audience, but there's no denying the infectious nature of enthusiasm. For instance, a watch manufacturer in New York conducted an experiment with two series of advertisements: one focused on the watch's technical superiority and features like construction, workmanship, and durability; the other emphasized the pride and pleasure of owning the watch. Surprisingly, the latter series outsold the former by double. Similarly, a salesman at a locomotive company noted that emotional appeal was more persuasive than highlighting mechanical excellence when selling railroad engines.

Countless examples underscore that our actions are often driven by emotions. Effective speakers understand this and strive to evoke strong feelings in their audience. Daniel Webster, renowned for his oratory skills, recognized that the true power of a speaker lies in their ability to stir emotions. He eloquently described eloquence as follows:

> 'Affected passion, intense expression, the pomp of declamation, all may aspire after it; they cannot reach it. It comes, if it come at all, like the outbreak of a fountain from the earth, or the bursting forth of volcanic fires, with spontaneous, original, native force.
>
> The graces taught in the schools, the costly ornaments and studied contrivances of speech, shock and disgust men, when their own lives, and the fate of their wives,

their children, and their country hang on the decision of the hour. Then words have lost their power, rhetoric is in vain, and all elaborate oratory contemptible. Even genius itself then feels rebuked and subdued, as in the presence of higher qualities. Then patriotism is eloquent, then self-devotion is eloquent. The clear conception outrunning the deductions of logic, the high purpose, the firm resolve, the dauntless spirit, speaking on the tongue, beaming from the eye, informing every feature, and urging the whole man onward, right onward to his subject—this, this is eloquence; or rather, it is something greater and higher than all eloquence; it is action, noble, sublime, godlike action.'

While traveling through the Northwest some time ago, I walked up a village street after dinner and noticed a crowd gathered around a speaker at a corner, standing on a goods-box. Intrigued by Emerson's advice to learn from every encounter, I stopped to listen to this speaker's pitch. He was peddling a hair tonic, claiming it was discovered in Arizona. Demonstrating its effects, he removed his hat to reveal his own hair, washed his face in the tonic to show its harmlessness, and passionately extolled its virtues. His enthusiasm was so infectious that half-dollars flowed into his hands like a silver flood from the enthralled audience.

After selling his tonic, he posed a question: why do more men than women go bald? When no one knew the answer, he confidently explained that it was due to women wearing thinner-soled shoes, which supposedly allowed them to absorb the earth's electrical energy. In contrast, men's thick-soled shoes blocked this vital energy, causing their hair to weaken and fall out. Naturally, he had a solution—a small copper plate to be nailed onto the shoe's sole. He painted a vivid picture of the benefits of avoiding baldness and praised the transformative powers of his copper plates.

Surprisingly, despite the outlandish nature of his claims, the speaker's fervor swept the audience along, and they eagerly crowded around him, clamoring to obtain these magical plates with outstretched quarters. Emerson's wisdom had been proven once again—the persuasive power of enthusiasm was truly remarkable!

Enthusiasm has driven millions to crusade for the Holy Land against the Saracens. It ignited Europe into a thirty-year war over religion. Enthusiasm propelled three small ships across uncharted seas to the shores of a new world. When Napoleon's weary army faltered in their ascent of the Alps, the Little Corporal halted them and commanded the bands to play the Marseillaise. Under its stirring melody, the daunting Alps seemed to vanish.

Emerson wisely stated, 'Nothing great was ever achieved without enthusiasm.' Carlyle affirmed that 'Every great movement in history has been the triumph of enthusiasm.' It spreads like wildfire—contagious as measles. Half of eloquence is inspiration. Sweep your audience along in the pulsating waves of enthusiasm. Let yourself be carried away. As Oliver Cromwell said, 'A man never rises so high as when he knows not whither he is going.'

But how do we cultivate and nurture this elusive quality of enthusiasm?

It cannot be put on like a smoking jacket, nor found in a book. It is a growth—an effect. But what causes it? Let's explore.

Emerson wrote:

> A painter told me that nobody could draw a tree without
> in some sort becoming a tree; or draw a child by studying

the outlines of his form merely,—but, by watching for a time his motion and plays, the painter enters his nature, and then can draw him at will in every attitude. So Roos 'entered into the inmost nature of his sheep.' I knew a draughtsman employed in a public survey, who found that he could not sketch the rocks until their geological structure was first explained to him.

When Sarah Bernhardt prepares for a challenging role, she isolates herself from four o'clock in the afternoon until after the performance, immersing herself completely in her character. Booth, as legend has it, forbade anyone from speaking to him between acts of his Shakespearean roles—he was Macbeth, not Booth. Dante, exiled and condemned to death, penned *The Divine Comedy* from the depths of his soul, living in caves and enduring starvation. Bunyan felt his *Pilgrim's Progress* so intensely that he once collapsed in tears of joy on the floor of Bedford jail. Turner, residing in a garret, trekked nine miles before dawn to witness the sunrise over the ocean, capturing its breathtaking beauty. Wendell Phillips' speeches crackled with 'silent lightning,' fueled by the anguish of five million slaves.

There's only one path to infuse genuine emotion into your speaking—remember this above all else: You must embody the character you portray, champion the cause you advocate, argue the case you present—immerse yourself so deeply that it consumes you entirely. In doing so, you align with your subject's essence, feeling what it feels, sharing its fervor, thus making your enthusiasm both authentic and contagious. The Carpenter who spoke as 'never man spake' delivered words fueled by a profound love for humanity—he had immersed himself in humanity, becoming one with Man.

But let's not view these words as a simple recipe for manufacturing emotion to serve an audience's whim. Genuine emotion in a speech is the very lifeblood of the speech itself, inseparable from its essence. In the perfect address, theme, speaker, and audience blend into one, united by the emotion and intellect of the moment.

The Importance of Empathy Towards Humanity

Emphasizing the speaker's need for a profound and wide-ranging compassion for human nature cannot be overstated. According to one of Victor Hugo's biographers, his prowess as both an orator and a writer stemmed from his expansive empathy and deep religious convictions. Recently, during a talk on short-story writing, the editor of Collier's Weekly underscored the critical nature of this broad love for humanity, almost apologizing for delivering what seemed like a sermon. Few, if any, immortal speeches have been delivered for selfish or narrow causes—they have always sprung from a fervent desire to uplift humanity. Examples include Paul's address to the Athenians on Mars Hill, Lincoln's Gettysburg Address, The Sermon on the Mount, and Henry's speech before the Virginia Convention of Delegates.

The hallmark of greatness is a genuine desire to serve others. While self-preservation is instinctual, selflessness defines true greatness—and art. Selfishness, identified as the root of all sin, is the target of all great religions and worthy philosophies. Speeches that truly move humanity emanate from hearts overflowing with genuine sympathy and love.

Former United States Senator Albert J. Beveridge in an introduction to one of the volumes of *Modern Eloquence*, says:

> The profoundest feeling among the masses, the most influential element in their character, is the religious

element. It is as instinctive and elemental as the law of self-preservation. It informs the whole intellect and personality of the people. And he who would greatly influence the people by uttering their unformed thoughts must have this great and unanalyzable bond of sympathy with them.

When the men of Ulster mobilized against the Home Rule Act, one of our team tasked a hundred men with preparing speeches on 'Home Rule.' Among them were seasoned lawyers and political campaigners, each offering a variety of well-informed and eloquent addresses. However, it was a humble clerk, lacking extensive education and experience, who captured the audience's hearts. He spoke of his childhood in Ulster, recounting tales of valor passed down by his mother and inspired by a painting in his uncle's home depicting Ulster's triumph over tyranny. With trembling voice and uplifted hand, he declared that if Ulster went to war, they would not be alone—a divine presence would be with them.

His speech stirred and electrified the audience, leaving a lasting impact. In contrast, the sophisticated speeches filled with lofty rhetoric and historical insights failed to resonate deeply. The clerk's genuine conviction and heartfelt connection to the topic not only moved his listeners but also garnered personal sympathy for the cause he championed.

As Webster wisely noted, authenticity in speech cannot be feigned successfully. 'Nature is forever putting a premium on reality.' Any falseness is quickly exposed. The thoughts and emotions that shape a speech in preparation must be genuinely felt and expressed on the platform. Consistency between words, voice, and demeanor is essential. There's no place for half-hearted or indifferent delivery methods. Sincerity, indeed, forms the very essence of eloquence.

Carlyle was right:

No Mirabeau, Napoleon, Burns, Cromwell, no man adequate to do anything, but is first of all in right earnest about it; what I call a sincere man. I should say sincerity, a great, deep, genuine sincerity, is the first characteristic of all men in any way heroic. Not the sincerity that calls itself sincere; ah no, that is a very poor matter indeed; a shallow braggart, conscious sincerity, oftenest self-conceit mainly. The great man's sincerity is of the kind he cannot speak of—is not conscious of.

9

Dealing with Drama

Under the vast expanse of the sky, there exists only one singular method to compel anyone to take action. Have you ever paused to ponder this truth? Yes, just one method exists, and that is by kindling within the other person the desire to act.

Bear in mind, there exists no alternative approach.

Certainly, you could compel someone to relinquish their watch by brandishing a revolver. You could coerce cooperation from your employees—albeit fleetingly—by threatening their jobs. You could enforce compliance from a child with a whip or a threat. Yet, these rudimentary tactics yield undesirable consequences.

The sole means by which I can prompt you to act is by fulfilling your desires.

What is it that you desire?

As Sigmund Freud posited, every action we undertake is propelled by two primary motives: the urge for intimacy and the aspiration for greatness.

John Dewey, one of America's most profound philosophers, expressed this idea in slightly different terms. Dr. Dewey stated that the deepest urge in human nature is 'the desire to be important.' This phrase—'the desire to be important'—holds immense significance. It is a concept you will encounter frequently throughout this book.

What do you truly want? While your list of desires may

not be extensive, the few things you do wish for, you crave with an unyielding insistence. Some of the primary desires that most people have include:

1. Health and the preservation of life
2. Food
3. Sleep
4. Money and the things money can buy
5. Life in the hereafter
6. Sexual gratification
7. The well-being of our children
8. A feeling of importance

Nearly all these desires are typically satisfied—except for one. There is a longing, almost as deep and as commanding as the desire for food or sleep, that is seldom fulfilled. This is what Freud referred to as 'the desire to be great,' and what Dewey termed 'the desire to be important.'

This need for a sense of importance is profound and often overlooked. People will go to great lengths to feel significant and valued. It drives our actions, influences our decisions, and shapes our interactions with others. Understanding this can transform the way you approach relationships, work, and life itself. If you can satisfy this need in others, you will unlock a powerful tool for motivation and influence. Remember, the desire to be important is not just a fleeting want—it is a fundamental human drive.

Abraham Lincoln once began a letter with the observation, 'Everybody likes a compliment.' William James echoed a similar sentiment when he remarked that 'the deepest principle in human nature is the craving to be appreciated.' James didn't just speak of a wish or a desire to be appreciated—he emphasized the word 'craving.'

This craving for appreciation is a profound and persistent human hunger. The rare individual who genuinely satisfies this need can wield tremendous influence and captivate others to such an extent that, as the saying goes, 'even the undertaker will be sorry when he dies.'

The desire for a sense of importance stands as one of the chief distinguishing features between mankind and animals. Allow me to illustrate this with a personal anecdote: During my youth on a farm in Missouri, my father bred fine Duroc-Jersey hogs and pedigreed white-faced cattle. We frequently showcased our livestock at country fairs and shows across the Midwest, where we won numerous first prizes. To commemorate these victories, my father would pin the blue ribbons on a sheet of white muslin. Whenever friends or visitors came to our house, he would proudly display this sheet, holding one end while I held the other, showcasing the blue ribbons.

The hogs themselves were indifferent to the ribbons and prizes they had won. But for my father, these accolades provided a profound sense of importance and achievement. They validated his efforts and made him feel recognized and esteemed—an experience deeply ingrained in human nature, far beyond the realm of mere animal instinct.

If our ancestors hadn't possessed this intense urge for a feeling of importance, civilization itself would have been inconceivable. Without it, we would have remained akin to mere animals.

This desire for significance was the driving force behind Dickens as he penned his timeless novels. It fueled Sir Christopher Wren's grand architectural visions in stone. It motivated Rockefeller to amass fortunes he never fully spent. And this same desire led the wealthiest families in towns across the globe to construct houses far larger than necessary for their needs.

This longing for importance permeates everyday life,

compelling individuals to seek the latest fashions, drive the newest cars, and proudly discuss the achievements of their children.

Throughout history, countless famous figures provide entertaining examples of their struggles for recognition. Even George Washington harbored a desire to be addressed as 'His Mightiness, the President of the United States,' while Columbus pleaded for the titles of 'Admiral of the Ocean' and 'Viceroy of India.' Catherine the Great insisted on only opening letters addressed to 'Her Imperial Majesty,' and Mrs. Lincoln, in the White House, famously confronted Mrs. Grant, demanding, 'How dare you be seated in my presence until I invite you!' These anecdotes underscore the powerful and sometimes amusing lengths to which individuals will go in pursuit of a sense of importance.

Appreciation as a Vital Psychological Need

Sometimes, individuals resort to physical or emotional ailments to garner sympathy, attention, and ultimately, a sense of importance. Consider Mrs. McKinley, who, as the wife of the President of the United States, found solace and validation in his constant presence by her side. She ensured his attention even during mundane activities like dental appointments, insisting he remain with her rather than fulfill important state obligations, such as meeting with his secretary of state, John Hay.

Mary Roberts Rinehart shared with me a poignant story of a vibrant young woman who, facing the stark realities of aging and loneliness, chose to become an invalid to satisfy her deep-seated need for significance. For a decade, she confined herself to bed, relying on her devoted elderly mother for constant care and attention. When her mother passed away, leaving her without her primary caretaker, the woman initially languished in despair. Yet, after a period of mourning, she summoned the strength to rise from her bed, reclaim her life, and reintegrate into society once more.

These examples illustrate the profound lengths to which individuals may go to fulfill their craving for recognition and significance, often through unconventional and sometimes drastic means.

The reasons why individuals may descend into insanity are complex and multifaceted, often defying simple explanations. While some cases can be linked to physical causes like brain lesions, alcohol abuse, toxins, or injuries that directly damage brain cells, there exists another perplexing category where no such organic abnormalities are found upon examination.

In these cases, where the brain tissue appears physically healthy, the causes of insanity delve into deeper psychological and emotional realms. It is suggested that profound psychological stress, unresolved trauma, intense emotional turmoil, and a lack of coping mechanisms may contribute significantly to mental instability.

Moreover, societal factors such as extreme social isolation, chronic stress, economic hardship, and the absence of supportive relationships can exacerbate these vulnerabilities. The human psyche's intricate workings and its susceptibility to breakdown under prolonged strain highlight the complexity of mental health issues.

Ultimately, the causes of insanity cannot be neatly categorized into one definitive answer; rather, they span a spectrum of biological, psychological, and environmental factors that interact in unique and often unpredictable ways in each individual case.

I posed this question to the chief physician of one of our nation's leading psychiatric institutions. This esteemed doctor, renowned for his expertise and accolades in the field, candidly admitted that the definitive causes of insanity remain elusive. It is a perplexing mystery that defies precise explanation. However, he did offer a profound insight into the phenomenon based on his clinical experience.

According to him, many individuals who descend into insanity seem to find within it a sense of significance and importance that eluded them in their everyday lives. He illustrated this with a poignant anecdote:

'There is a patient under my care currently whose life has been marked by tragedy. She yearned for love, intimacy, children, and social status, but her reality was starkly different. Her marriage turned out to be a bitter disappointment. Her husband not only failed to love her but also isolated her, demanding she serve his meals upstairs alone. She never had children and lacked any social standing. Eventually, she succumbed to insanity.'

'In her delusions, she has divorced her husband in her mind and reclaimed her maiden name. Now, she firmly believes she has married into English aristocracy and insists on being addressed as Lady Smith. Furthermore, she imagines giving birth to a new child every night, eagerly telling me during each visit, "Doctor, I had a baby last night."'

In her shattered reality, where all her aspirations were dashed against the harsh cliffs of life's hardships, the world of insanity has become a refuge—a place where her dreams sail triumphantly into safe harbors under billowing sails and the joyful chorus of winds.

The physician's perspective on the patient's happiness in her delusions offers a striking insight: sometimes, what appears tragic from the outside may hold a deeper contentment for the individual involved. If some individuals are driven to insanity by their intense hunger for significance, then consider the transformative power we possess by offering genuine appreciation in our daily interactions.

Just as we provide nourishment for the body through meals of roast beef and potatoes, we must also nourish the self-esteem of our loved ones, friends, and colleagues. Kind words of appreciation have the potential to resonate in their hearts for years, akin to the celestial melody of morning stars.

Flattery, however, rarely succeeds with discerning individuals. It often comes across as shallow, self-serving, and insincere, destined to fail in its intended purpose. While some may be so starved for recognition that they accept any form of praise, even Queen Victoria herself fell prey to flattery. Prime Minister Disraeli famously admitted to 'spreading it on with a trowel' in his dealings with her, though his polished charm suited his context and role far better than it would for most of us.

In the end, flattery is akin to counterfeit currency; it might provide temporary gain but carries the risk of eventual exposure and harm if relied upon habitually. Genuine appreciation, however, is the authentic currency of human connection, fostering lasting bonds and enriching lives in ways that superficial praise can never match.

The distinction between appreciation and flattery is clear-cut. Appreciation is sincere, emanating genuinely from the heart, while flattery is insincere, superficial, and often motivated by selfish intentions. Genuine appreciation is universally respected for its authenticity, whereas flattery is universally condemned for its deceitfulness.

I recall visiting Chapultepec palace in Mexico City where I encountered a bust of General Álvaro Obregón, beneath which were inscribed these insightful words from his philosophy: 'Don't be afraid of enemies who attack you. Be afraid of friends who flatter you.' This wisdom underscores the danger of insincere praise.

Let me be unequivocal: I am not advocating for flattery. Quite the contrary, I am advocating for a transformative approach to life. King George V exemplified this with a maxim displayed in his study at Buckingham Palace: 'Teach me neither to proffer nor receive cheap praise.' Flattery, after all, is nothing more than cheap praise, as succinctly defined in a quote I once read: 'Flattery is telling the other person precisely what he thinks about himself.'

Ralph Waldo Emerson captured a profound truth when he said, 'Use what language you will, you can never say anything but what you are.' This reminds us that our words reflect our character and integrity, distinguishing between genuine appreciation that uplifts and flattery that deceives.

If our goal were simply to flatter, everyone would quickly catch on, and we would all consider ourselves experts in human relations. However, genuine human connection and effective communication go beyond mere flattery.

Much of our time, when not occupied with specific tasks, is spent introspectively, thinking about ourselves. Yet, if we shift our focus momentarily away from ourselves and instead recognize the positive qualities of others, we can avoid resorting to insincere flattery that rings hollow the moment it leaves our lips.

One of the most overlooked virtues in daily life is appreciation. Often, we forget to praise our children when they excel, whether it's bringing home a good report card or accomplishing their first baking or carpentry project. Children thrive on parental interest and approval, finding nothing more pleasing than receiving recognition for their efforts.

Consider expressing appreciation in other contexts as well. For instance, if you enjoy a well-prepared filet mignon at a club, sending compliments to the chef acknowledges their skill and effort. Similarly, when a tired salesperson treats you with exceptional courtesy, a simple acknowledgment of their efforts can make a significant difference.

Professionals across various fields—ministers, lecturers, public speakers—often experience the disappointment of pouring their hearts out to an audience without receiving any appreciative feedback. This sentiment is magnified for workers in offices, shops, factories, and even within our own families and social circles. In our interactions with others, it's crucial to remember that everyone, regardless of their role, craves and deserves appreciation. It serves as a universal form of recognition and validation that enriches our connections with one another.

Try sprinkling small sparks of gratitude along your daily path. You'll be amazed at how these sparks ignite tiny flames of friendship that become guiding beacons on your future journeys.

In a workplace scenario in New Fairfield, Connecticut, Pamela Dunham faced the challenge of supervising a janitor who was performing poorly. His work was so subpar that it not only invited ridicule from colleagues but also disrupted productivity in the shop. Despite various attempts to motivate him, including criticisms and demonstrations of his shortcomings, Pam found no success.

However, Pam noticed occasional instances where the janitor performed exceptionally well. Instead of dwelling on his failures, she decided to praise his good work publicly in front of his peers. Gradually, day by day, his overall performance improved. Encouraged by the honest appreciation he received, he began to take pride in his work and soon became efficient in all his tasks. Now, he consistently delivers excellent results and earns the appreciation and respect of his colleagues.

This story illustrates how genuine appreciation can achieve what criticism and ridicule often cannot. It shows the transformative power of recognition and how it can inspire positive change and foster a supportive work environment.

Hurting people not only fails to change them; it is never

justified. There's an age-old maxim that I've affixed to my mirror, ensuring I confront it daily: 'I shall pass this way but once; any good, therefore, that I can do or any kindness that I can show to any human being, let me do it now. Let me not defer nor neglect it, for I shall not pass this way again.' Ralph Waldo Emerson once reflected, 'Every man I meet is my superior in some way. In that, I learn of him.' If this was Emerson's perspective, isn't it likely to be even more applicable to each of us? Let's shift our focus away from our own achievements and desires. Instead, let's endeavor to recognize the positive qualities in others. Let's abandon flattery and offer genuine, heartfelt appreciation. Be generous in your approval and lavish in your praise, for such sincere words will be cherished, treasured, and remembered long after they're spoken—echoing through lifetimes, even when we ourselves have forgotten them.

10

Summoning Storms and Avoiding Foes

When Theodore Roosevelt occupied the White House, he openly admitted that achieving accuracy in his decisions seventy-five percent of the time would meet his highest expectations. If such a distinguished figure could aim for this standard, what about the rest of us?

Consider this: if you can be right just fifty-five percent of the time, you could step onto Wall Street and potentially earn a million dollars a day. But if you can't even reach that modest level of certainty, why should you assert others are wrong?

Critiquing someone's views can be done just as effectively through a glance, a tone, or a gesture as through words. And when you tell someone they are wrong directly, it doesn't invite agreement—it often triggers defensiveness. You inadvertently strike at their intelligence, judgment, pride, and self-respect, which only fuels resistance. No amount of logical argument, no matter how profound, can sway their opinions once their feelings are hurt.

Therefore, never begin a discussion with a declaration like, 'I am going to prove this to you.' Such an approach immediately sets up a confrontational dynamic, implying superiority and an intent to impose your viewpoint. Instead, why not create a more receptive atmosphere? Changing minds is challenging even in the best circumstances, so why make it more difficult? Why start at a disadvantage?

Harold Reinke, a Dodge dealer in Billings, Montana, found a transformative approach in his dealings with customers. Recognizing the toll that a hardened and callous demeanor was taking on customer relations and business outcomes, he decided to pivot. Instead of escalating conflicts with defensive responses, he adopted a more humble and open stance.

In his own words to his class, Reinke described his new approach: 'Our dealership has made so many mistakes that I am frequently ashamed. We have erred in your case. Tell me about it.' This simple acknowledgment of fallibility and readiness to listen marked a significant shift in his interactions.

Reinke understood that defusing tension and showing genuine willingness to address concerns could foster better relationships and smoother resolutions. His experience underscores the power of humility and openness in customer service—a lesson that transcends industries and contexts.

'This approach proves remarkably disarming. By the time customers express their grievances, they often become more receptive to resolving the issue amicably. In fact, several customers have expressed gratitude for my understanding attitude. Two even brought friends to purchase new cars. In this fiercely competitive market, cultivating more of these customer interactions is crucial. Respect for all opinions and diplomatic, courteous treatment can give us a competitive edge.'

Admitting the possibility of being wrong is a surefire way to prevent disputes and encourage fairness from opponents. It prompts them to consider their own openness and broadmindedness. On the other hand, if you assert someone is wrong without tact, the consequences can be severe. Take Mr. S, a young New York attorney who argued a pivotal case before the United States Supreme Court (Lustgarten v. Fleet Corporation 280 U.S. 320). When challenged by a justice on a legal point, Mr. S responded bluntly, asserting there was no statute of limitations in admiralty law.

'As I recounted to one of the author's classes,' Mr. S recalled, 'a hush fell over the court, and the room grew icy. I knew I was right, and the justice was wrong. But my direct approach did not win him over. Despite my belief in the law and my impassioned argument, I made a critical mistake by telling a highly respected and learned man that he was mistaken.'

Few people operate purely on logic; our minds are often clouded by prejudices, biases, and entrenched beliefs. As Carl Rogers, the renowned psychologist, noted in his book *On Becoming a Person*:

'I have found it immensely valuable when I allow myself to truly understand others. The wording of this statement might sound peculiar. Do we need to give ourselves permission to understand another person? I believe we do. Our initial response to most statements from others tends to be evaluation or judgment rather than genuine understanding. When someone expresses a feeling, attitude, or belief, our instinct is often to think, "that's right," "that's stupid," "that's abnormal," "that's unreasonable," "that's incorrect," or "that's not nice." Rarely do we truly attempt to grasp the precise meaning of their statement from their perspective.'

Reflecting on personal experiences, I once engaged an interior decorator to create draperies for my home. When the bill arrived, I was taken aback. Later, when a friend visited and commented on the price, she exclaimed triumphantly, 'What? That's terrible. I think he took advantage of you.'

Was she right? Yes, she spoke the truth, but few enjoy hearing truths that question their judgment. Human nature being what it is, I found myself defending the decision, arguing that quality and artistic taste come at a cost and justifying my expenditure.

The following day, another friend visited, admired the draperies, and enthusiastically expressed her desire for similar creations in her own home. In response, my perspective shifted entirely. 'Honestly,' I confessed, 'I can't afford them myself. I paid too much. I regret ordering them.'

In these instances, reactions were shaped not just by facts but by the emotional responses and biases inherent in human nature.

When we realize we are wrong, we may admit it to ourselves. If handled gently and tactfully, we might even admit it to others, finding pride in our honesty and open-mindedness. However, being forced to swallow an unpalatable truth by someone else is rarely effective.

Horace Greeley, America's most prominent editor during the Civil War era, vehemently opposed Lincoln's policies. He believed he could bend Lincoln to his will through relentless argument, ridicule, and abuse. Month after month, year after year, he waged a bitter campaign against Lincoln, culminating in a scathing, personal attack on the President the very night Booth assassinated him.

Did Greeley's bitterness persuade Lincoln to agree with him? Not in the least. Ridicule and abuse, as history shows, seldom change minds.

Diplomacy Opens Doors

For excellent advice on managing people, self-improvement, and developing a refined personality, consider reading Benjamin Franklin's autobiography—one of the most captivating life stories in American literature. Franklin recounts how he overcame his argumentative tendencies to become one of the most adept, polished, and diplomatic figures in American history.

As a young and tactless youth, Franklin received a sharp rebuke from an old Quaker friend who said something like:

'Ben, you are impossible. Your opinions offend everyone who disagrees with you. People enjoy themselves more when you're not around. You think you know everything, so no one bothers to enlighten you. Thus, you are unlikely to ever learn more than you already know, which is very little.'

This honest criticism was a turning point for Franklin, prompting him to reflect on his approach and ultimately transform into a more diplomatic and respected figure.

One of the most admirable qualities of Ben Franklin was his ability to accept a stinging rebuke with grace and wisdom. He recognized its truth and foresaw the path to potential failure and social ruin. Thus, he swiftly made a profound change in his behavior.

'I made a rule,' Franklin reflected, 'to refrain from directly contradicting others' opinions and from asserting my own with unwavering certainty. I even prohibited myself from using words that implied fixed beliefs, such as "certainly" or "undoubtedly." Instead, I adopted phrases like "I conceive," "I apprehend," or "it appears to me at present" when expressing my views. When confronted with someone else's erroneous assertion, I disciplined myself not to bluntly contradict them or immediately point out flaws in their argument. Instead, I began by acknowledging that their opinion might be valid in certain cases, but in the current context, I perceived differences.'

Franklin soon realized the benefits of this approach. Conversations became more harmonious, and my modest presentation of opinions led to greater acceptance and less opposition. I experienced less embarrassment when proven wrong and found it easier to persuade others to abandon their errors and align with my views when I was correct.

'This method, initially adopted against my natural inclinations, eventually became so natural and habitual that for the past fifty years, perhaps no one has heard a dogmatic statement from me. This habit, along with my reputation for integrity, contributed significantly to my influence among fellow citizens when proposing new institutions or reforms in existing ones. Despite being a mediocre speaker with a tendency to hesitate and stumble over words, I often succeeded in gaining support for my proposals in public councils.'

How does Franklin's approach translate to business? Consider these examples:

Katherine A. Allred, an industrial engineering supervisor from Kings Mountain, North Carolina, oversees operations at a yarn-processing plant. She shared with our class how her approach to a sensitive issue evolved before and after she adopted Franklin's principles:

'As part of my role, I am responsible for implementing and maintaining incentive systems for our operators to increase yarn production and earnings. Our existing system worked well with a limited range of yarn types, but as we expanded to over twelve varieties, it became inadequate. I developed a new system that would pay operators based on the type of yarn they processed at any given time. Armed with my new approach, I went into a meeting determined to prove its superiority. I pointed out flaws in the current system and insisted that my solution was flawless. Needless to say, I failed miserably. By defending my position so vigorously, I left no room for management to gracefully acknowledge the shortcomings of the old system. The discussion stalled, and no progress was made.'

'After several sessions of this course, I came to recognize where I had gone wrong. I called another meeting and this time I asked the team where they perceived the challenges with our current approach. We discussed each point openly, and I sought their opinions on the best path forward. With subtle suggestions at appropriate moments, I guided them towards developing my proposed system themselves. By the end of the meeting, when I formally presented my system, they embraced it enthusiastically.'

'I am now firmly convinced that directly telling someone they are wrong achieves nothing positive and often damages relationships. It strips them of their dignity and makes productive discussion nearly impossible.'

Consider another example, typical of the experiences shared by many. R. V. Crowley, a salesman for a lumber company in New York, reflected on his own approach:

'I used to confront hard-nosed lumber inspectors for years, adamantly insisting they were wrong—and often winning those arguments. Yet, it never changed anything. These inspectors were as steadfast in their decisions as baseball umpires. Once made, their rulings rarely budged.'

Mr. Crowley realized these confrontations were costing his firm thousands of dollars. During my course, he resolved to change tactics and abandon combative arguments. The results were telling, as he recounted to his classmates:

'One morning, I received a call from an agitated person claiming the lumber we had shipped was entirely unsatisfactory. Their firm had halted unloading and demanded we retrieve the stock from their yard. Their inspector reported significant discrepancies in grade, citing a fifty-five percent shortfall. Normally, I would have cited grading rules and argued from my own experience to defend our product. Instead, I decided to apply the principles I had learned.'

'When I arrived at the plant, I found the purchasing agent and the lumber inspector in a contentious mood, ready for a confrontation. We proceeded to the car being unloaded, and I requested that they continue while I observed closely. I asked the inspector to segregate the rejects as usual and place the acceptable pieces in a separate pile.

'As I watched, it became apparent to me that the inspector's standards were overly stringent and that he was misapplying the grading rules, especially since this lumber was white pine—an area where my expertise surpassed his. Despite knowing he was grading incorrectly, I refrained from challenging him directly. Instead, I asked questions in a cooperative manner, seeking to understand why certain pieces didn't meet their standards. My only intention, I emphasized, was to ensure future shipments aligned perfectly with their requirements.

'By maintaining a friendly and collaborative approach, and consistently affirming their right to reject boards that didn't meet their needs, I gradually warmed him up and thawed the tension between us. Occasionally, I subtly hinted that some of the rejected pieces might actually fall within their purchased grade but without making it a contentious issue.

'His attitude slowly shifted. He eventually admitted his lack of experience with white pine and began seeking my guidance on each piece as it was unloaded. I explained why certain pieces met their specified grade, always emphasizing that we didn't want them to accept anything unsuitable for their purposes. Eventually, he started feeling guilty about placing pieces in the reject pile and realized that their initial specifications may not have matched their actual needs.

'In the end, he re-evaluated the entire carload after I left, accepted the entire shipment, and we received full payment.

'This single instance underscored the power of tact and the decision not to confront someone directly about being wrong. It not only saved my company a significant amount of money but also preserved invaluable goodwill that is hard to quantify.'

Martin Luther King, Jr., once explained his admiration for Air Force General Daniel 'Chappie' James, despite being a pacifist, by stating, 'I judge people by their own principles—not by my own.'

In a similar vein, General Robert E. Lee demonstrated a profound approach to leadership when he spoke highly of an officer who was known to be one of his staunchest critics. When questioned about this, Lee replied, 'The president asked my opinion of him, not his opinion of me.'

This wisdom echoes timeless advice found in various cultures throughout history. Jesus Christ, two thousand years ago, advised, 'Agree with thine adversary quickly.' Even earlier, Pharaoh Akhtoi of Egypt, over two thousand years before Christ, counselled his son with pragmatic wisdom: 'Be diplomatic; it will help you gain your point.'

In essence, the lesson remains clear: in dealings with others—whether customers, spouses, or adversaries—avoiding argumentation, refraining from declaring them wrong, and employing diplomacy can be remarkably effective strategies.

11

The Warp Device

It is often the case among those focused on practical matters that imagination is undervalued in comparison to direct, straightforward thinking. Emerson's assertion that 'Science does not know its debt to the imagination' may be dismissed by such individuals as the musings of a speculative essayist, a philosopher, or a poet. However, when Napoleon, renowned for his strategic acumen, declares that 'The human race is governed by its imagination,' his words carry weight and command respect.

It should be acknowledged that the ability to form mental images is a crucial component of the mind's machinery. While it must complement pure thought, the synergy between imagination and rationality often yields significant outcomes for human happiness and well-being. As we delve deeper into this topic, the profound impact of imagination in various spheres should become increasingly evident.

What is Imagination?

Rather than attempting a definitive definition—given the multitude of interpretations available—let us focus on understanding imagination as either the faculty or the process of creating mental images.

Imagination engages with subject matter that can be real, entirely fantastical, or a blend of both. Whether it pertains to the physical realm, the spiritual domain, or both, the mental image crafted by imagination is simultaneously unrestrained yet bound by certain principles—a paradoxical offspring of the mind.

Primarily, as implied by its name, imagination operates as a process. Here, memory plays a crucial role, serving as the foundation upon which imaginative constructs are built.

Reproductive Imagination

The ability to see, hear, feel, taste, or smell something fleeting and transient, only to be able to conjure it again at will, is what we call reproductive imagination. Two main factors influence how vividly we can recreate these mental images: the intensity of the original experience and the individual's capacity for mental reproduction. Every normal person possesses some degree of clarity in evoking these images.

The variation in the strength of this imaging faculty among individuals holds significant implications for anyone studying public speaking. Those lacking in poetic impulses may not aspire to be poets, yet many with seemingly dormant imaging faculties aspire to be effective public speakers. To these individuals, we earnestly advise: awaken your ability to create mental images, for even in the most logically structured discourse, this skill proves invaluable. It is crucial to assess promptly the depth and reliability of your imagination, as it can be cultivated or misused.

Francis Galton notes that the French excel in visualizing, evident in their meticulous planning of ceremonies and their strategic prowess. Their ingenuity in technical innovations and clarity in expression further attest to this ability. Conversely, individuals differ significantly in this regard, much like the contrast between the Dutch and the French. This disparity exists not only among those deemed imaginative or unimaginative by their peers but also among those whose talents or habits are less known.

Let us now experiment with six well-known types of mental imaging to observe how they manifest in our minds:

(a) **Visual Image:** Most common is the ability to recall scenes visually, often termed as being 'eye-minded' by psychologists. Picture the scene around your breakfast table this morning. Though it may not have been memorable, recall a striking table scene from your past, vividly etched due to its strong impression on you.

(b) **Auditory Image:** Following visual images, auditory recollections are quite vivid. Block out external stimuli and imagine the distinct sound of thunder among rocky mountains or the tearing of ropes under strain. Engage with sounds that evoke real sensations in your mind.

(c) **Motor Image:** Similar in intensity to auditory images, motor imagery involves recalling physical sensations. Remember the strain of exertion against an immovable object in your sleep or the sudden jolt of a moving vehicle. These memories evoke visceral responses.

(d) **Gustatory Image:** Recollections related to taste are also potent. The thought of biting into a lemon or savoring a memorable meal can induce physical reactions such as salivation or distaste.

(e) **Olfactory Image:** More delicate still are olfactory images, capable of triggering strong emotional responses. Some may feel nauseated by memories of unpleasant odors, while others relish the reminiscence of delightful scents.

(f) **Tactile Image:** Finally, tactile memories can be equally powerful. Recall the sensation of velvet under your fingertips, the burn of touching a cold stove, or the comforting touch of a loved one's hand.

These images rarely exist in isolation but often combine to form complex, multi-sensory recollections—like the sight and sound of an avalanche or the flash and report of a gunshot.

Productive Imagination

The examples and experiments previously mentioned focus on reproductive imagination. While these can be pleasurable or horrific, they are less significant than the images evoked by productive imagination. This distinction does not imply a separate faculty but highlights a different aspect of imagination.

Consider a scene you once witnessed on a street corner, where you saw the beginning but not the conclusion. Recalling the initial part is an exercise in reproductive imagination. However, imagining what happened next—allowing your fantasy to fill in the gaps—is an exercise in productive imagination. Here, you consciously invent the unreal based on the real.

The fictionist, poet, and public speaker will recognize the value of productive imagery. While the foundation of their creations is grounded in reality, their aspirations and ideas soar, blending the tangible with the intangible.

One critical point is that imagery is most valuable when controlled by the higher intellectual power of pure reason. An untutored mind may confuse the real with the unreal, valuing both equally. In contrast, a trained mind distinguishes between the two and evaluates each appropriately. Unrestrained imaging can be like a rudderless steamer, while a trained faculty is like a graceful sloop, navigating smoothly with reason at the helm and imagination catching every breeze.

Productive imagination is essential in various fields: a chess game, a warlord's tactical plan, a geometrical theorem, a business campaign, factory efficiency, a powerful drama, overcoming economic obstacles, crafting a sublime poem, or convincing an audience. Each of these achievements starts as an image, transforming into reality through careful planning and imagination. Just as a farmer must envision a harvest beyond the seeds, one must cultivate creative imagination, building 'what might be' upon the foundation of 'what is.'

The Uses of Imaging in Public Speaking

By now, you may have already started applying these ideas to public speaking, but let's delve into some specific uses.

I. Imaging in Speech Preparation

(a) **Set the image of your audience before you while you prepare.** You can't anticipate every reaction, but it's essential to visualize your audience. Consider their probable mood and attitude toward the occasion, the theme, and you as the speaker.

(b) **Conceive your speech as a whole while you are preparing its parts.** Visualize how each part fits together. This holistic view helps in creating a cohesive and compelling speech.

(c) **Image the language you will use.** Whether your speech is written or extemporaneous, imagining the language will help you select varied figures of speech. Fresh comparisons are crucial; a speech without them is like a garden without blooms. Avoid hackneyed phrases and let your imagination craft vivid, original comparisons.

For example, observe the fresh and effective description in the opening of O. Henry's story, *The Harbinger*:

> Long before the springtide is felt in the dull bosom of the yokel does the city man know that the grass-green goddess is upon her throne. He sits at his breakfast eggs and toast, begirt by stone walls, opens his morning paper and sees journalism leave vernalism at the post.
>
> For whereas Spring's couriers were once the evidence of our finer senses, now the Associated Press does the trick.
>
> The warble of the first robin in Hackensack, the stirring of the maple sap in Bennington, the budding of the pussy willows along the main street in Syracuse, the first chirp of the bluebird, the swansong of the blue point, the annual tornado in St. Louis, the plaint of the peace pessimist from Pompton, N.J., the regular visit of the tame wild goose with a broken leg to the pond near Bilgewater Junction, the base attempt of the Drug Trust to boost the price of quinine foiled in the House by Congressman Jinks, the first tall poplar struck by lightning and the usual stunned picnickers who had taken refuge, the first crack of the ice jamb in the Allegheny River, the finding of a violet in its mossy bed by the correspondent at Round Corners—these are the advanced signs of the burgeoning season that are wired into the wise city, while the farmer sees nothing but winter upon his dreary fields.
>
> But these be mere externals. The true harbinger is the heart. When Strephon seeks his Chloe, and Mike his Maggie, then only is Spring arrived and the newspaper report of the five-foot rattler killed in Squire Pettregrew's pasture confirmed.

A hackneyed writer might have simply said that newspapers inform city dwellers about spring before farmers see any evidence, and that love is the real harbinger of spring, quoting, "In the Spring a young man's fancy lightly turns to thoughts of love." Instead, O. Henry's imagery vividly brings the scene to life.

By using such imaginative language, you can captivate your audience and make your message more memorable and impactful.

II. Imaging in Speech Delivery

When the passion of speech takes hold of you and you are fully engaged, your mood will become one of vision. At this point:

(a) Re-image past emotions. Recall the feelings you experienced during significant moments. Like an actor reliving emotions with every performance, bring those old feelings to life in your speech.

(b) Reconstruct the scenes you describe. Visualize and recreate in your mind the scenes you are narrating to your audience.

(c) Image the objects in nature whose tone you are delineating. Let your bearing, voice, and movement (gesture) vividly convey the scene. Instead of merely stating that whiskey ruins homes, the temperance speaker should paint a vivid picture of a drunkard coming home, abusing his wife, and striking his children. This is far more effective than abstract statements. To depict the cruelty of war, show a soldier with an arm severed by a shell, lying on the battlefield pleading for water; show children with tear-stained faces praying for their deceased father to return. Avoid general and prosaic terms. Paint pictures. Create images for your audience's imagination to build into their own mental visuals.

III. How to Acquire the Imaging Habit

Consider the American statesman who said, 'The way to resume is to resume.' The application here is clear: begin practicing image-making as outlined in this chapter.

(a) **Test your qualities of image-making**: One by one, practice creating different types of images.
(b) **Combine images**: Many images come to us in complex forms, such as the combined noise, shoving, and hot odor of a cheering crowd. Practice combining images to enhance your mental imagery.
(c) **Practice reproductive imaging**: Start by reproducing images from your memory and then move on to productive imaging by adding creative elements to these images. This cultivates invention.
(d) **Let your imagination roam freely**: Occasionally, allow yourself to create complete imaginary scenes—sights, sounds, and scenarios. The world of fantasy is open for exploration.
(e) **Train yourself in figurative language**: Learn to distinguish and use various forms of figurative language. When used with restraint, tropes can be highly effective. However, beware of letting extravagance creep in, as it can diminish the power of your speech.
(f) **Master your images—do not let them master you.** By practicing and honing these techniques, you can develop a habit of effective imaging, enhancing your public speaking skills and making your presentations more vivid and compelling.

12

Banishing Worries

As a child growing up on a Missouri farm, I was often plagued by fears and worries. One day, while helping my mother pit cherries, I began to cry. She asked, 'Dale, what in the world are you crying about?' Through my tears, I blurted out, 'I'm afraid I am going to be buried alive!'

In those days, my worries were numerous. Thunderstorms terrified me as I feared being struck by lightning. Hard times made me anxious about having enough food to eat. I fretted about going to hell after I died. I was also terrified that an older boy, Sam White, would cut off my big ears as he had threatened. I worried about being laughed at by girls if I tipped my hat to them and feared that no girl would ever want to marry me. I even worried about what I would say to my wife immediately after our wedding. I pictured us getting married in a country church and riding back to the farm in a surrey with fringe on top, but I was anxious about how to keep the conversation going during that ride.

As the years passed, I gradually realized that ninety-nine percent of the things I worried about never happened. For example, I was once terrified of lightning, but I now know that the chances of being killed by lightning in any given year are, according to the National Safety Council, only one in three hundred and fifty thousand.

My fear of being buried alive was even more irrational. Even before embalming became standard practice, the likelihood of being buried alive was probably less than one in ten million. Yet, I once cried over this fear.

Statistics show that one person out of every eight dies of cancer. If I had wanted a legitimate worry, I should have focused on cancer instead of lightning or being buried alive.

While these examples reflect the worries of my youth and adolescence, many adult worries are equally absurd. If we paused to consider the law of averages, you and I could likely eliminate nine-tenths of our current worries by realizing that most of them have no real justification.

The Law of Averages

Lloyd's of London, the world's most renowned insurance company, has made a fortune capitalizing on people's tendency to worry about unlikely disasters. Lloyd's essentially bets that the calamities people fear will not occur, although they call it insurance rather than betting. This betting is grounded in the law of averages, and Lloyd's has been thriving for over two centuries. Given human nature's inclination towards irrational fears, it will likely continue to prosper for millennia, insuring everything from shoes to ships against disasters that, statistically, are much rarer than people imagine.

General George Crook, arguably the greatest fighter in American history, observed in his autobiography that 'nearly all the worries and unhappiness' of the Indians stemmed from their imagination rather than reality. Reflecting on my own life, I realize that my worries often followed the same pattern. This insight is shared by Jim Grant, owner of the James A. Grant Distributing Company in New York City. He frequently ordered large quantities of Florida oranges and grapefruit and would torment himself with concerns like: What if there's a train wreck? What if my fruit is scattered across the countryside? What if a bridge collapses while my cars are crossing it?

Although his fruit was insured, Jim feared that failing to deliver on time could cost him his market. His constant worrying led him to believe he had stomach ulcers, so he visited a doctor. The diagnosis? Just jumpy nerves. This revelation made him reconsider his anxieties. He asked himself: 'Jim Grant, how many fruit cars have you handled over the years?' The answer: 'About twenty-five thousand.' Then he asked: 'How many of those cars were ever wrecked?' The answer: 'Maybe five.' This meant that only five out of twenty-five thousand cars had been wrecked, a ratio of five thousand to one. According to the law of averages, the chances of one of his cars being wrecked were five thousand to one. So why worry?

The lesson here is clear: many of our fears are unfounded when viewed through the lens of the law of averages. Recognizing this can significantly reduce our worries and improve our peace of mind.

'Then I said to myself: "Well, a bridge may collapse!" Then I asked myself: "How many cars have you actually lost from a bridge collapsing?' The answer was—"None." Then I said to myself: "Aren't you a fool to be worrying yourself into stomach ulcers over a bridge which has never yet collapsed, and over a railroad wreck when the chances are five thousand to one against it!" 'When I looked at it that way,' Jim Grant told me, 'I felt pretty silly. I decided then and there to let the law of averages do the worrying for me—and I have not been troubled with my "stomach ulcer" since!'

When Al Smith was Governor of New York, I heard him respond to his political critics by repeatedly saying: 'Let's examine the record... let's examine the record.' He would then present the facts. The next time you and I find ourselves worrying about what might happen, let's take a cue from wise old Al Smith: 'let's examine the record and see what basis there is, if any, for our gnawing anxieties.' This is precisely what Frederick J. Mahlstedt did when he feared he was lying in his grave. Here is his story as he told it to one of our adult-education classes in New York:

'Early in June, 1944, I was lying in a slit trench near Omaha Beach. I was with the 999th Signal Service Company, and we had just 'dug in' in Normandy. As I looked around at that slit trench—just a rectangular hole in the ground—I said to myself, 'This looks just like a grave.' When I lay down and tried to sleep in it, it felt like a grave. I couldn't help saying to myself, 'Maybe this is my grave.' When the German bombers began coming over at 11 p.m., and the bombs started falling, I was scared stiff. For the first two or three nights I couldn't sleep at all. By the fourth or fifth night, I was almost a nervous wreck. I knew that if I didn't do something, I would go stark crazy. So I reminded myself that five nights had passed, and I was still alive; and so was every man in our outfit. Only two had even been injured, and they had been hurt, not by German bombs, but by falling flak from our own antiaircraft guns.

I decided to stop worrying by doing something constructive. So I built a thick wooden roof over my slit trench to protect myself from flak. I thought of the vast area over which my unit was spread. I told myself that the only way I could be killed in that deep, narrow slit trench was by a direct hit; and I figured out that the chance of a direct hit on me was not one in ten thousand. After a couple of nights of looking at it in this way, I calmed down and slept even through the bomb raids!'

13

Optimizing Existence

Look out the window. Notice how much change has occurred out there in just the past few years. The postwar boom went bust. Competition became global. Consumers grew more sophisticated. Quality became an expectation. Whole new industries were born, and others were realigned. Some dried up and blew away. The idea of two military superpowers now seems like ancient history. The Eastern Bloc fell apart. Europe is growing more unified by the day. The Third World countries are trying to elbow their way onto the economic stage. Most of the cushiness has gone out of modern capitalism—and with it the blessed stability that generations of business people had come to expect.

Did Dale Carnegie anticipate every one of these changes? Of course not. No one could have in a world changing so fast. But Carnegie did something even more important. He left behind a timeless set of human-relations principles that are just as relevant today as they ever were. And as things turned out, they are uniquely suited to the current high-stress, fast-moving, uncertain world.

Look at things from the other person's perspective. Offer genuine appreciation and praise. Harness the mighty power of enthusiasm. Respect the dignity of others. Don't be overly critical. Give people a good reputation to live up to. Keep a sense of fun and balance in your life.

Three generations of students and business people have benefited from this essential wisdom. More people are benefiting every day.

The timelessness of Carnegie's principles should come as no surprise. They were never rooted in the realities of any particular moment, realities that are guaranteed to change and change. Carnegie tested his principles too long and hard for that. Fads would come and go over the years. Stocks would rise and fall. Technology would accelerate ahead. Political parties would win and lose. And the economic pendulum would swing like a hypnotist's watch—good times, bad times, good times, bad times…

But Carnegie's insights were solid. They merely needed to be applied. They were built around basic facts of human nature, so their essential truth never waned. They worked when the world was humming along. In this new era of constant change, they work just as well. Only now the need for Carnegie's principles—for anything that works—is greater than it's ever been.

So apply these basic lessons and techniques. Make them part of your daily life. Use them with your friends, family, and colleagues. See what a difference they can make.

The Carnegie principles don't require an advanced degree in human psychology. They don't call for years of reflection and thought. All they take is practice, energy, and a real desire to get along better in the world.

'The rules we have set down here are not mere theories or guesswork,' Dale Carnegie said about the principles he spent his life teaching to millions. 'They work like magic. Incredible as it sounds, I have seen the application of these principles literally revolutionize the lives of many people.'

So take those words to heart, and find the leader in you. Embrace these timeless principles, for they are not bound by fleeting trends but grounded in enduring truths of human interaction. Use them consistently, and watch as they transform your relationships and opportunities, making you a more effective leader in today's dynamic world.